Standards Practice Book

For Home or School

Grade 2

INCLUDES:

- Home or School Practice
- Lesson Practice and Test Preparation
- English and Spanish School-Home Letters
- Getting Ready for Grade 3 Lessons

Number Sense and Place Value

Critical Area Extending understanding of base-ten notation

1 Number Concepts

Domains Operations and Algebraic Thinking
Number and Operations in Base Ten
Common Core Standards 2.OA.3, 2.NBT.2, 2.NBT.3

School-Home Letter (English) **P1**
School-Home Letter (Spanish). **P2**
1.1 **Hands On: Algebra** • Even and Odd Numbers **P3**
1.2 **Algebra** • Represent Even Numbers. **P5**
1.3 Understand Place Value. **P7**
1.4 Expanded Form **P9**
1.5 Different Ways to Write Numbers. **P11**
1.6 **Algebra** • Different Names for Numbers **P13**
1.7 **Problem Solving** • Tens and Ones **P15**
1.8 Counting Patterns Within 100 . . . . **P17**
1.9 Counting Patterns Within 1,000 . . . . **P19**

2 Numbers to 1,000

Domains Number and Operations in Base Ten
Common Core Standards 2.NBT.1, 2.NBT.1a, 2.NBT.1b, 2.NBT.3, 2.NBT.4, 2.NBT.8

School-Home Letter (English) **P21**
School-Home Letter (Spanish). **P22**
2.1 Group Tens as Hundreds **P23**
2.2 Explore 3-Digit Numbers **P25**
2.3 **Hands On** • Model 3-Digit Numbers. **P27**
2.4 Hundreds, Tens, and Ones **P29**
2.5 Place Value to 1,000 . . . . **P31**
2.6 Number Names **P33**
2.7 Different Forms of Numbers **P35**
2.8 **Algebra** • Different Ways to Show Numbers **P37**
2.9 Count On and Count Back by 10 and 100 . . . . **P39**
2.10 **Algebra** • Number Patterns **P41**
2.11 **Problem Solving** • Compare Numbers **P43**
2.12 **Algebra** • Compare Numbers **P45**

CRITICAL AREA: Addition and Subtraction

COMMON CORE   **Critical Area** Building fluency with addition and subtraction

3   Basic Facts and Relationships

Domains Operations and Algebraic Thinking
Common Core Standards 2.OA.1, 2.OA.2, 2.OA.4

	School-Home Letter (English)	P47
	School-Home Letter (Spanish)	P48
3.1	Use Doubles Facts	P49
3.2	Practice Addition Facts	P51
3.3	**Algebra** • Make a Ten to Add	P53
3.4	**Algebra** • Add 3 Addends	P55
3.5	**Algebra** • Relate Addition and Subtraction	P57
3.6	Practice Subtraction Facts	P59
3.7	Use Ten to Subtract	P61
3.8	**Algebra** • Use Drawings to Represent Problems	P63
3.9	**Algebra** • Use Equations to Represent Problems	P65
3.10	**Problem Solving** • Equal Groups	P67
3.11	**Algebra** • Repeated Addition	P69

4   2-Digit Addition

Domains Operations and Algebraic Thinking
        Number and Operations in Base Ten
Common Core Standards 2.OA.1, 2.NBT.5, 2.NBT.6

	School-Home Letter (English)	P71
	School-Home Letter (Spanish)	P72
4.1	Break Apart Ones to Add	P73
4.2	Use Compensation	P75
4.3	Break Apart Addends as Tens and Ones	P77
4.4	Model Regrouping for Addition	P79
4.5	Model and Record 2-Digit Addition	P81
4.6	2-Digit Addition	P83
4.7	Practice 2-Digit Addition	P85
4.8	Rewrite 2-Digit Addition	P87
4.9	**Problem Solving** • Addition	P89
4.10	**Algebra** • Write Equations to Represent Addition	P91
4.11	**Algebra** • Find Sums for 3 Addends	P93
4.12	**Algebra** • Find Sums for 4 Addends	P95

5 2-Digit Subtraction

Domains Operations and Algebraic Thinking
Number and Operations in Base Ten
Common Core Standards 2.OA.1, 2.NBT.5

School-Home Letter (English) **P97**
School-Home Letter (Spanish) **P98**
5.1 **Algebra** • Break Apart Ones to Subtract **P99**
5.2 **Algebra** • Break Apart Numbers to Subtract **P101**
5.3 Model Regrouping for Subtraction **P103**
5.4 Model and Record 2-Digit Subtraction **P105**
5.5 2-Digit Subtraction **P107**
5.6 Practice 2-Digit Subtraction **P109**
5.7 Rewrite 2-Digit Subtraction **P111**
5.8 Add to Find Differences **P113**
5.9 **Problem Solving** • Subtraction **P115**
5.10 **Algebra** • Write Equations to Represent Subtraction **P117**
5.11 Solve Multistep Problems **P119**

6 3-Digit Addition and Subtraction

Domains Number and Operations in Base Ten
Common Core Standards 2.NBT.7

School-Home Letter (English) **P121**
School-Home Letter (Spanish) **P122**
6.1 Draw to Represent 3-Digit Addition **P123**
6.2 Break Apart 3-Digit Addends **P125**
6.3 3-Digit Addition: Regroup Ones **P127**
6.4 3-Digit Addition: Regroup Tens **P129**
6.5 Addition: Regroup Ones and Tens **P131**
6.6 Estimation in 3-Digit Addition **P133**
6.7 **Problem Solving** • 3-Digit Subtraction **P135**
6.8 3-Digit Subtraction: Regroup Tens **P137**
6.9 3-Digit Subtraction: Regroup Hundreds **P139**
6.10 Subtraction: Regroup Hundreds and Tens **P141**
6.11 Regrouping with Zeros **P143**
6.12 Estimation in 3-Digit Subtraction **P145**

CRITICAL AREA # Measurement and Data

COMMON CORE **Critical Area** Using standard units of measure

7 Money and Time

Domains Measurement and Data
Common Core Standards 2.MD.7, 2.MD.8

	School-Home Letter (English)	P147
	School-Home Letter (Spanish)	P148
7.1	Dimes, Nickels, and Pennies	P149
7.2	Quarters	P151
7.3	Count Collections	P153
7.4	**Hands On** • Show Amounts in Two Ways	P155
7.5	One Dollar	P157
7.6	Amounts Greater Than $1	P159
7.7	**Problem Solving** • Money	P161
7.8	Time to the Hour and Half Hour	P163
7.9	Time to 5 Minutes	P165
7.10	Practice Telling Time	P167
7.11	A.M. and P.M.	P169
7.12	Units of Time	P171

8 Length in Customary Units

Domains Measurement and Data
Common Core Standards 2.MD.1, 2.MD.2, 2.MD.3, 2.MD.5, 2.MD.6, 2.MD.9

	School-Home Letter (English)	P173
	School-Home Letter (Spanish)	P174
8.1	**Hands On** • Measure With Inch Models	P175
8.2	**Hands On** • Make and Use a Ruler	P177
8.3	Estimate Lengths in Inches	P179
8.4	**Hands On** • Measure with an Inch Ruler	P181
8.5	**Problem Solving** • Add and Subtract in Inches	P183
8.6	**Hands On** • Measure in Inches and Feet	P185
8.7	Estimate Lengths in Feet	P187
8.8	Choose a Tool	P189
8.9	Display Measurement Data	P191

9 Length in Metric Units

Domains Measurement and Data
Common Core Standards 2.MD.1, 2.MD.2, 2.MD.3, 2.MD.4, 2.MD.5, 2.MD.6

	School-Home Letter (English)	**P193**
	School-Home Letter (Spanish).	**P194**
9.1	**Hands On** • Measure with a Centimeter Model	**P195**
9.2	Estimate Lengths in Centimeters	**P197**
9.3	**Hands On** • Measure with a Centimeter Ruler	**P199**
9.4	**Problem Solving** • Add and Subtract Lengths	**P201**
9.5	**Hands On** • Centimeters and Meters	**P203**
9.6	Estimate Lengths in Meters	**P205**
9.7	**Hands On** • Measure and Compare Lengths	**P207**

10 Data

Domains Measurement and Data
Common Core Standards 2.MD.10

	School-Home Letter (English)	**P209**
	School-Home Letter (Spanish).	**P210**
10.1	Collect Data.	**P211**
10.2	Read Picture Graphs	**P213**
10.3	Make Picture Graphs	**P215**
10.4	Read Bar Graphs	**P217**
10.5	Make Bar Graphs	**P219**
10.6	**Problem Solving** • Display Data	**P221**

Geometry and Fractions

COMMON CORE **Critical Area** Describing and analyzing shapes

 Geometry and Fraction Concepts

Domains Geometry
Common Core Standards 2.G.1, 2.G.2, 2.G.3

	School-Home Letter (English)	**P223**
	School-Home Letter (Spanish)	**P224**
11.1	Three-Dimensional Shapes	**P225**
11.2	Attributes of Three-Dimensional Shapes	**P227**
11.3	**Hands On** • Build Three-Dimensional Shapes	**P229**
11.4	Two-Dimensional Shapes	**P231**
11.5	Angles in Two-Dimensional Shapes	**P233**
11.6	Sort Two-Dimensional Shapes	**P235**
11.7	**Hands On** • Partition Rectangles	**P237**
11.8	Equal Parts	**P239**
11.9	Show Equal Parts of a Whole	**P241**
11.10	Describe Equal Parts	**P243**
11.11	**Problem Solving** • Equal Shares	**P245**

End-of-Year Resources

Getting Ready for Grade 3

These lessons review important skills and prepare you for Grade 3.

Lesson 1   Find Sums on an Addition Table **P247**

Lesson 2   Estimate Sums: 2-Digit Addition **P249**

Lesson 3   Estimate Sums: 3-Digit Addition **P251**

Lesson 4   Estimate Differences: 2-Digit Subtraction **P253**

Lesson 5   Estimate Differences: 3-Digit Subtraction **P255**

Lesson 6   Order 3-Digit Numbers **P257**

Checkpoint **P259**

Lesson 7   Equal Groups of 2 . . . . **P261**

Lesson 8   Equal Groups of 5 . . . . **P263**

Lesson 9   Equal Groups of 10 . . . . **P265**

Lesson 10   **Hands On:** Size of Shares **P267**

Lesson 11   **Hands On:** Number of Equal Shares **P269**

Lesson 12   Solve Problems with Equal Shares **P271**

Checkpoint **P273**

Lesson 13   Hour Before and Hour After **P275**

Lesson 14   Elapsed Time in Hours **P277**

Lesson 15   Elapsed Time in Minutes **P279**

Lesson 16   **Hands On:** Capacity • Nonstandard Units **P281**

Lesson 17   Describe Measurement Data **P283**

Checkpoint **P285**

Lesson 18   Fraction Models: Thirds and Sixths **P287**

Lesson 19   Fraction Models: Fourths and Eighths **P289**

Lesson 20   Compare Fraction Models **P291**

Checkpoint **P293**

School-Home Letter

Dear Family,

My class started Chapter 1 this week. In this chapter, I will learn about place value of 2-digit numbers and even and odd numbers.

Love, _____

Vocabulary

digits 0, 1, 2, 3, 4, 5, 6, 7, 8, and 9 are digits.

even numbers 2, 4, 6, 8, 10 . . .

odd numbers 1, 3, 5, 7, 9 . . .

Home Activity

Give your child a group of 20 small objects, such as beans. Have your child count the objects and tell how many. Then have your child pair the objects and tell whether the number is *even* or *odd*. Repeat with a different number of beans.

Literature

Look for this book at the library. Ask your child to point out math vocabulary words as you read the book together.

One Hundred Hungry Ants by Elinor J. Pinczes. Houghton Mifflin, 1993.

Querida familia:

Mi clase comenzó el Capítulo 1 esta semana. En este capítulo, aprenderé sobre el valor posicional de los números de 2 dígitos y números pares e impares.

Con cariño, _____

Vocabulario

dígitos 0, 1, 2, 3, 4, 5, 6, 7, 8 y 9 son dígitos.

números pares 2, 4, 6, 8, 10 . . .

números impares 1, 3, 5, 7, 9 . . .

Actividad para la casa

Dé a su hijo un grupo de 20 objetos pequeños, como unos frijoles. Pídale que cuente los objetos y que diga cuántos hay. Luego, pídale que los agrupe y diga si el número es *par* o *impar*. Repita con un número distinto de frijoles.

Literatura

Busque este libro en la biblioteca. Pídale a su hijo que señale palabras del vocabulario de matemáticas mientras leen juntos el libro.

One Hundred Hungry Ants
por Elinor J. Pinczes.
Houghton Mifflin, 1993.

Algebra • Even and Odd Numbers

COMMON CORE STANDARD— 2.OA.3
Work with equal groups of objects to gain foundations for multiplication.

Shade in the ten frames to show the number. Circle even or odd.

1.   15

even   odd

2.   18

even   odd

3.   11

even   odd

4.   17

even   odd

5.   13

even   odd

6.   20

even   odd

Problem Solving Real World

7. Mr. Dell has an odd number of sheep and an even number of cows on his farm. Circle the choice that could tell about his farm.

9 sheep and 10 cows

10 sheep and 11 cows

8 sheep and 12 cows

Lesson Check (2.OA.3)

1. Circle the even number.

3

4

5

9

2. Circle the odd number.

2

6

7

8

Spiral Review (2.OA.3)

3. Circle the odd number.

10

8

3

4

4. Circle the even number.

7

6

5

1

5. Circle the even number.

9

7

5

2

6. Circle the odd number.

1

4

8

10

Algebra • Represent Even Numbers

COMMON CORE STANDARD—2.OA.3
Work with equal groups of objects to gain foundations for multiplication.

Shade in the frames to show two equal groups for each number. Complete the addition sentence to show the groups.

1. 8

___ = ___ + ___

2. 18

___ = ___ + ___

3. 10

___ = ___ + ___

4. 14

___ = ___ + ___

5. 20

___ = ___ + ___

6. 12

___ = ___ + ___

Problem Solving

Solve. Write or draw to explain.

7. The seats in a van are in pairs. There are 16 seats. How many pairs of seats are there?

_____ pairs of seats

Lesson Check (2.OA.3)

1. Circle the sum that is an even number.

$9 + 9 = 18$

$9 + 8 = 17$

$8 + 7 = 15$

$6 + 5 = 11$

2. Circle the sum that is an even number.

$1 + 2 = 3$

$3 + 3 = 6$

$2 + 5 = 7$

$4 + 7 = 11$

Spiral Review (2.OA.3)

3. Circle the even number.

7

9

10

13

4. Circle the odd number.

4

11

16

20

5. Ray has an odd number of cats. He also has an even number of dogs. Complete the sentence.

Ray has _____ cats and

_____ dogs.

6. Circle the sum that is an even number.

$2 + 3 = 5$

$3 + 4 = 7$

$4 + 4 = 8$

$7 + 8 = 15$

Understand Place Value

COMMON CORE STANDARD—2.NBT.3
Understand place value.

Circle the value of the underlined digit.

1. 2̲3

20   2

2. 4̲8

8   80

3. 1̲8

10   1

4. 4̲3

40   4

5. 5̲4

5   50

6. 65̲

50   5

7. 7̲0

7   70

8. 37̲

70   7

9. 2̲2

20   2

Problem Solving

Write the 2-digit number that matches the clues.

10. My number has a tens digit that is 8 more than the ones digit. Zero is not one of my digits.

My number is _____.

Lesson Check (2.NBT.3)

1. What is the value of the underlined digit? Write the number.

3<u>2</u>

_____

2. What is the value of the underlined digit? Write the number.

<u>2</u>8

_____

Spiral Review (2.OA.3, 2.NBT.3)

3. What is the value of the underlined digit? Write the number.

<u>5</u>3

_____

4. What is the value of the underlined digit? Write the number.

2<u>4</u>

_____

5. Is the number of pens and pencils together even or odd? Write the number. Circle even or odd.

2 pens + 3 pencils _____ total

even   odd

6. Circle the sum that is an even number.

$5 + 2 =$ _____

$6 + 3 =$ _____

$7 + 4 =$ _____

$7 + 7 =$ _____

Expanded Form

COMMON CORE STANDARD—2.NBT.3
Understand place value.

Draw a quick picture to show the number.
Describe the number in two ways.

1. 68

_____ tens _____ ones

_____ + _____

2. 21

_____ tens _____ one

_____ + _____

3. 70

_____ tens _____ ones

_____ + _____

4. 53

_____ tens _____ ones

_____ + _____

5. 35

_____ tens _____ ones

_____ + _____

6. 47

_____ tens _____ ones

_____ + _____

Problem Solving

7. Circle the ways to write the
number shown by the model.

| 4 tens 6 ones | 40 + 6 | 64 |
| 6 tens 4 ones | 60 + 4 | 46 |

Lesson Check (2.NBT.3)

1. Describe the number 92 in tens and ones.

_____ tens _____ ones

2. Describe the number 45 in tens and ones.

_____ tens _____ ones

Spiral Review (2.NBT.3)

3. What is the value of the underlined digit? Write the number.

4̲9

_____

4. What is the value of the underlined digit? Write the number.

34̲

_____

5. Describe the number 76 in another way.

||||||| ∘∘∘∘∘∘

_____ tens _____ ones

6. Describe the number 52 in another way.

||||| ∘∘

_____ tens _____ ones

Different Ways to Write Numbers

COMMON CORE STANDARD—2.NBT.3
Understand place value.

Write the number another way.

1. 32

_____ tens _____ ones

2. forty-one

_____

3. 9 tens 5 ones

_____

4. 80 + 3

_____

5. 57

_____ tens _____ ones

6. seventy-two

_____ + _____

7. 60 + 4

_____

8. 4 tens 8 ones

_____

9. twenty-eight

_____ + _____

10. 80

_____ tens _____ ones

Problem Solving

11. A number has the digit 3 in the ones place and the digit 4 in the tens place. Which of these is another way to write this number? Circle it.

3 + 4   40 + 3   30 + 4

Lesson Check (2.NBT.3)

1. Write 3 tens 9 ones in another way.

_____

2. Write the number eighteen in another way.

_____

Spiral Review (2.NBT.3)

3. Write the number 47 in tens and ones.

_____ tens _____ ones

4. Write the number 95 in words.

_____

5. What is the value of the underlined digit? Write the number.

6<u>1</u>

_____

6. What is the value of the underlined digit? Write the number.

<u>1</u>7

_____

Algebra • Different Names for Numbers

COMMON CORE STANDARD—2.NBT.3
Understand place value.

The blocks show the number in different ways.
Describe the blocks in two ways.

1. 24

_____ tens _____ ones

_____ + _____

_____ ten _____ ones

_____ + _____

_____ tens _____ ones

_____ + _____

2. 36

_____ tens _____ ones

_____ + _____

_____ ten _____ ones

_____ + _____

_____ tens _____ ones

_____ + _____

3. 45

_____ tens _____ ones

_____ + _____

_____ tens _____ ones

_____ + _____

_____ tens _____ ones

_____ + _____

Problem Solving

4. Toni has these blocks. Circle
the blocks that she could use
to show 34.

Lesson Check (2.NBT.3)

1. What number is shown with the blocks? Write the number.

2 tens 13 ones

_____

2. What number is shown with the blocks? Write the number.

1 ten 16 ones

_____

Spiral Review (2.NBT.3)

3. What number is shown with the blocks? Write the number.

1 ten 17 ones

_____

4. What is the value of the underlined digit? Write the number.

2<u>9</u>

_____

5. Which is another way to write 9 tens 3 ones? Write the number.

_____

6. Describe the number 50 in tens and ones.

_____ tens _____ ones

Problem Solving • Tens and Ones

COMMON CORE STANDARD—2.NBT.3
Understand place value.

Find a pattern to solve.

1. Ann is grouping 38 rocks. She can put them into groups of 10 rocks or as single rocks. What are the different ways Ann can group the rocks?

Groups of 10 rocks	Single rocks

2. Mr. Grant needs 30 pieces of felt. He can buy them in packs of 10 or as single pieces. What are the different ways Mr. Grant can buy the felt?

Packs of 10 pieces	Single pieces

3. Ms. Sims is putting away 22 books. She can put them on the table in stacks of 10 or as single books. What are the different ways Ms. Sims can put away the books?

Stacks of 10 books	Single books

Lesson Check (2.NBT.3)

1. Mrs. Chang is packing 38 apples. She can pack them in bags of 10 or as single apples. Complete the table to show another way Mrs. Chang can pack the apples.

Bags of 10 apples	Single apples
2	18
1	28
0	38

Spiral Review (2.NBT.3)

2. What is the value of the underlined digit? Write the number.

   5̲4

   _____

3. What number is shown with the blocks? Write the number.

   2 tens 19 ones

   _____

4. Write the number 62 in words.

   _____

5. What number can be written as 8 tens and 6 ones? Write the number.

   _____

Counting Patterns Within 100

COMMON CORE STANDARD—2.NBT.2
Understand place value.

Count by ones.

1. 58, 59, _____, _____, _____, _____, _____

Count by fives.

2. 45, 50, _____, _____, _____, _____, _____

3. 20, 25, _____, _____, _____, _____, _____

Count by tens.

4. 20, _____, _____, _____, _____, _____, _____

Count back by ones.

5. 87, 86, 85, _____, _____, _____

Problem Solving

6. Tim counts his friends' fingers by fives.
   He counts six hands. What numbers does he say?

   5, _____, _____, _____, _____, _____

Lesson Check (2.NBT.2)

1. Count by fives.

70, _____, _____, _____, _____

2. Count by tens.

60, _____, _____, _____, _____

Spiral Review (2.OA.3, 2.NBT.2, 2.NBT.3)

3. Count back by ones.

21, _____, _____, _____, _____

4. A number has 2 tens and 15 ones. Write the number in words.

_____

5. Describe the number 72 in tens and ones.

_____ tens _____ ones

6. Find the sum. Is the sum even or odd? Write even or odd.

$9 + 9 =$ _____

_____

Counting Patterns Within 1,000

COMMON CORE STANDARD—2.NBT.2
Understand place value.

Count by fives.

1. 415, 420, _____, _____, _____, _____

2. 675, 680, _____, _____, _____, _____, _____

Count by tens.

3. 210, 220, _____, _____, _____, _____, _____

4. 840, 850, _____, _____, _____, _____, _____

Count by hundreds.

5. 300, 400, _____, _____, _____, _____, _____

Count back by ones.

6. 953, 952, _____, _____, _____, _____, _____

Problem Solving

7. Lee has a jar of 100 pennies.
   She adds groups of 10 pennies to the jar.
   She adds 5 groups. What numbers does she say?

   _____, _____, _____, _____, _____

Lesson Check (2.NBT.2)

1. Count by tens.

160, ____, ____, ____, ____

2. Count by hundreds.

400, ____, ____, ____, ____

Spiral Review (2.NBT.2, 2.NBT.3)

3. Count by fives.

245, ____, ____, ____, ____

4. Count back by ones.

71, ____, ____, ____, ____

5. Describe 45 in another way.

____ tens ____ ones

6. Describe 7 tens 9 ones in another way.

_____

School-Home Letter

Dear Family,

My class started Chapter 2 this week. I will learn about place value of numbers to 1,000. I will also learn about comparing these numbers.

Love, _____

Vocabulary

compare To describe whether numbers are equal to, less than, or greater than one another

hundred A group of 10 tens

is equal to 145 is equal to 145

= 145 = 145

is greater than 131 is greater than 121

> 131 > 121

is less than 125 is less than 185

< 125 < 185

thousand A group of 10 hundreds

Home Activity

Have your child look through magazines for 3-digit numbers and cut them out. Work together to write a word problem using two of these numbers, gluing the cut-out numbers in place. Have your child solve the problem.

Charles collected __127__ leaves. Ann collected __240__ leaves. Who collected the greater number of leaves?

Literature

Reading math stories reinforces learning. Look for these books in the library.

A Place for Zero by Angeline Sparagna LoPresti and Phyllis Hornung. Charlesbridge Publishing, 2003.

More or Less by Stuart J. Murphy. HarperCollins, 2005.

Carta
para la casa

Querida familia:

Mi clase comenzó el Capítulo 2 esta semana. Aprenderé sobre el valor posicional de los números hasta 1,000. También aprenderé a comparar estos números.

Con cariño, _____

Vocabulario

comparar Describir si los números son iguales a, menores que o mayores que otro número

centena Un grupo de 10 decenas

es igual a 145 es igual a 145

= 145 = 145

es mayor que 131 es mayor que 121

> 131 > 121

es menor que 125 es menor que 185

< 125 < 185

millar Un grupo de 10 centenas

Actividad para la casa

Pídale a su hijo que busque números de 3 dígitos en revistas y que los recorte. Luego, trabajen juntos para escribir un problema usando dos de estos números y péguenlos en algún lugar. Pídale a su hijo que resuelva el problema.

Carlos juntó __127__ hojas.
Ana juntó __240__ hojas.
¿Quién juntó el mayor número de hojas?

Literatura

Leer cuentos de matemáticas refuerza el aprendizaje. Busque estos libros en la biblioteca.

A Place for Zero
por Angeline Sparagna LoPresti and Phyllis Hornung. Charlesbridge Publishing, 2003.

More or Less
por Stuart J. Murphy HarperCollins, 2005.

Group Tens as Hundreds

COMMON CORE STANDARDs—
2.NBT.1.A, 2.NBT.1.B
Understand place value.

**Write how many tens. Circle groups of 10 tens.
Write how many hundreds. Write the number.**

1. _____ tens

   _____ hundreds

   _____

2. _____ tens

   _____ hundreds

   _____

3. _____ tens

   _____ hundreds

   _____

Problem Solving

Solve. Write or draw to explain.

4. Farmer Gray has 30 flowerpots.
   He plants 10 seeds in each pot.
   How many seeds does he plant?

   _____ seeds

Lesson Check (2.NBT.1a, 2.NBT.1b)

1. Mai has 40 tens. Write how many hundreds. Write the number.

_____

_____

2. There are 80 tens. Write how many hundreds. Write the number.

_____

_____

Spiral Review (2.0A.3, 2.NBT.2, 2.NBT.3)

3. Write the number equal to 5 tens and 13 ones.

_____

4. Count by fives.

5, 10, 15

_____, _____, _____, _____

5. Carlos has 58 pencils. What is the value of the digit 5 in this number?

_____

6. Circle the sum that is an even number.

$2 + 3 = 5$

$4 + 4 = 8$

$5 + 6 = 11$

$8 + 7 = 15$

Explore 3-Digit Numbers

COMMON CORE STANDARD—2.NBT.1
Understand place value.

Circle tens to make 1 hundred. Write the number in different ways.

1.

_____ tens

_____ hundred _____ tens

_____

2.

_____ tens

_____ hundred _____ tens

_____

3.

_____ tens

_____ hundred _____ tens

_____

Problem Solving Real World

Solve. Write or draw to explain.

4. Millie has a box of 1 hundred cubes.
She also has a bag of 70 cubes.
How many trains of 10 cubes
can she make?

_____ trains of 10 cubes

Lesson Check (2.NBT.1)

1. Circle tens to make I hundred. Write the number a different way.

_____ tens

_____ hundred

_____ tens

_____

2. Circle tens to make I hundred. Write the number a different way.

_____ tens

_____ hundred

_____ tens

_____

Spiral Review (2.OA.3, 2.NBT.3)

3. Circle the odd number.

18   10

9   4

4. Write the number equal to 2 tens 15 ones.

_____

5. Describe the number 78 in two different ways.

_____ tens + _____ ones

_____ + _____

6. Write the number 55 in another way.

_____

Name _____

Model 3-Digit Numbers

COMMON CORE STANDARD—2.NBT.1
Understand place value.

Write how many hundreds, tens, and ones.
Show with ▦ ▬ ₒ. Then draw a quick picture.

1. 118

Hundreds	Tens	Ones

2. 246

Hundreds	Tens	Ones

3. 143

Hundreds	Tens	Ones

4. 237

Hundreds	Tens	Ones

 Problem Solving Real World

5. Write the number that matches the clues.

- My number has 2 hundreds.
- The tens digit is 9 more than the ones digit.

My number is _____.

Hundreds	Tens	Ones

Lesson Check (2.NBT.1)

1. What number is shown with these blocks?

Hundreds	Tens	Ones

_____

Spiral Review (2.OA.3, 2.NBT.1a, 2.NBT.1b, 2.NBT.3)

2. Write the number with the same value as 28 tens.

_____

3. Describe 59 in two other ways.

_____ tens _____ ones

_____ + _____

4. Circle the odd number.

11   12

18   20

5. Write the number equal to 7 tens and 3 ones.

_____

Hundreds, Tens, and Ones

COMMON CORE STANDARD—2.NBT.1, 2.NBT.3 Understand place value.

Write how many hundreds, tens, and ones are in the model. Write the number in two ways.

1.

Hundreds	Tens	Ones

_____

_____ + _____ + _____

2.

Hundreds	Tens	Ones

_____

_____ + _____ + _____

3.

Hundreds	Tens	Ones

_____

_____ + _____ + _____

Problem Solving Real World

4. Write the number that answers the riddle. Use the chart. A model for my number has 6 ones blocks, 2 hundreds blocks, and 3 tens blocks. What number am I?

Hundreds	Tens	Ones

_____

Lesson Check (2.NBT.1)

1. Write the number 254 as a sum of hundreds, tens, and ones.

_____ + _____ + _____

2. Write the number 307 as a sum of hundreds, tens, and ones.

_____ + _____ + _____

Spiral Review (2.OA.3, 2.NBT.1a, 2.NBT.1b, 2.NBT.3)

3. Describe 83 in two other ways.

_____ tens _____ ones

_____ + _____

4. Write 86 in words.

_____

5. Write the number with the same value as 32 tens.

_____

6. Circle the odd number.

2   6

10   17

Place Value to 1,000

COMMON CORE STANDARD—2.NBT.1
Understand place value.

Circle the value or the meaning of the underlined digit.

1. 33<u>7</u>	3	30	300
2. 46<u>2</u>	200	20	2
3. <u>5</u>72	5	50	500
4. 56<u>7</u>	7 ones	7 tens	7 hundreds
5. <u>4</u>62	4 hundreds	4 ones	4 tens
6. <u>1</u>,000	1 ten	1 hundred	1 thousand

Problem Solving

7. Write the 3-digit number that answers the riddle.

- I have the same hundreds digit as ones digit.
- The value of my tens digit is 50.
- The value of my ones digit is 4.   The number is _____.

Lesson Check (2.NBT.1)

1. What is the value of the underlined digit?

$$\underline{3}15$$

_____

2. What is the meaning of the underlined digit?

$$64\underline{8}$$

_____ tens

Spiral Review (2.OA.3, 2.NBT.1, 2.NBT.3)

3. What number can be written as $40 + 5$?

_____

4. What number has the same value as 14 tens?

_____

5. Write the number described by 1 ten 16 ones.

_____

6. Circle the even number.

| 7 | 16 |
| 21 | 25 |

Number Names

COMMON CORE STANDARD—2.NBT.3
Understand place value.

Write the number.

1. two hundred thirty-two

_____

2. five hundred forty-four

_____

3. one hundred fifty-eight

_____

4. nine hundred fifty

_____

5. four hundred twenty

_____

6. six hundred seventy-eight

_____

Write the number using words.

7. 317

_____

8. 457

_____

Problem Solving

Circle the answer.

9. Six hundred twenty-six children
attend Elm Street School. Which
is another way to write this number?

266   626   662

Lesson Check (2.NBT.3)

1. Write the number 851 in words.

_____

2. Write the number two hundred sixty using numbers.

_____

Spiral Review (2.NBT.1, 2.NBT.2)

3. Write a number with the digit 8 in the tens place.

_____

4. Write the number shown with these blocks.

_____

5. Count by fives.

650, 655,

____, ____, ____

6. Sam has 128 marbles. How many hundreds are in this number?

____ hundred

Different Forms of Numbers

COMMON CORE STANDARD—2.NBT.3
Understand place value.

**Read the number and draw a quick picture.
Then write the number in different ways.**

1. two hundred fifty-one

_____ hundreds _____ tens _____ one

_____ + _____ + _____

_____

2. three hundred twelve

_____ hundreds _____ ten _____ ones

_____ + _____ + _____

_____

3. two hundred seven

_____ hundreds _____ tens _____ ones

_____ + _____ + _____

_____

 Problem Solving *Real World*

Write the number another way.

4. 200 + 30 + 7

_____

5. 895

_____

Lesson Check (2.NBT.3)

1. Write the number 392 as hundreds, tens, and ones.

_____ hundreds _____ tens _____ ones

2. What is another way to write the number 271?

_____ hundreds _____ tens _____ one

Spiral Review (2.NBT.1, 2.NBT.3)

3. What is the value of the underlined digit?

5<u>6</u>

_____

4. What number is shown with these blocks?

_____

5. What is another way to write the number 75?

_____ + _____

6. What number can be written as 60 + 3?

_____

Algebra • Different Ways to Show Numbers

COMMON CORE STANDARD—2.NBT.3
Understand place value.

Write how many hundreds, tens, and ones are in the model.

1. 135

Hundreds	Tens	Ones

Hundreds	Tens	Ones

2. 216

Hundreds	Tens	Ones

Hundreds	Tens	Ones

Problem Solving *Real World*

Markers are sold in boxes, packs, or as single markers.
Each box has 10 packs. Each pack has 10 markers.

3. Draw pictures to show two ways
to buy 276 markers.

Lesson Check (2.NBT.3)

1. Write the number that can be shown with this many hundreds, tens, and ones.

Hundreds	Tens	Ones
1	2	18

_____

2. Write the number that can be shown with this many hundreds, tens, and ones.

Hundreds	Tens	Ones
2	15	6

_____

Spiral Review (2.NBT.3)

3. What number can be written as 6 tens 2 ones?

_____

4. What number can be written as 30 + 2?

_____

5. Write the number 584 in words.

_____

6. Write the number 29 in words.

_____

Count On and Count Back by 10 and 100

COMMON CORE STANDARD—2.NBT.8
Use place value understanding and properties of operations to add and subtract.

Write the number.

1. 10 more than 451

_____

2. 10 less than 770

_____

3. 100 more than 367

_____

4. 100 less than 895

_____

5. 10 less than 812

_____

6. 100 more than 543

_____

7. 10 more than 218

_____

8. 100 more than 379

_____

9. 100 less than 324

_____

10. 10 less than 829

_____

Problem Solving

Solve. Write or draw to explain.

11. Sarah has 128 stickers. Alex has 10 fewer stickers than Sarah. How many stickers does Alex have?

_____ stickers

Lesson Check (2.NBT.8)

1. Write the number that is 10 less than 526.

_____

2. Write the number that is 100 more than 487.

_____

Spiral Review (2.NBT.1, 2.NBT.3)

3. Write another way to describe 14 tens.

_____ hundred _____ tens

4. What is the value of the underlined digit?

5<u>8</u>7

_____

5. What number can be written as 30 + 5?

_____

6. What number can be written as 9 tens and 1 one?

_____

Algebra • Number Patterns

COMMON CORE STANDARD—2.NBT.8
Use place value understanding and properties
of operations to add and subtract.

Look at the digits to find the next two numbers.

1. 232, 242, 252, 262, , ☐

The next two numbers are _____ and _____.

2. 185, 285, 385, 485, ☐, ☐

The next two numbers are _____ and _____.

3. 428, 528, 628, 728, ☐, ☐

The next two numbers are _____ and _____.

4. 654, 664, 674, 684, ☐, ☐

The next two numbers are _____ and _____.

5. 333, 433, 533, 633, ☐, ☐

The next two numbers are _____ and _____.

Problem Solving

6. What are the missing numbers in the pattern?

431, 441, 451, 461, ☐, 481, 491, ☐

The missing numbers are _____ and _____.

Lesson Check (2.NBT.8)

1. What is the next number in this pattern?

453, 463, 473, 483,

_____

2. What is the next number in this pattern?

295, 395, 495, 595,

_____

Spiral Review (2.NBT.1, 2.NBT.3)

3. Write the number seven hundred fifty-one with digits.

_____

4. What is the value of the underlined digit?

_195

_____

5. What is another way to write 56?

_____ tens _____ ones

6. Write the number 43 in tens and ones.

_____ tens _____ ones

Name _____

Problem Solving • Compare Numbers

COMMON CORE STANDARD—2.NBT.4
Understand place value.

Model the numbers. Draw quick pictures to show how you solved the problem.

1. Lauryn has 128 marbles. Kristin has 118 marbles. Who has more marbles?

   _____

2. Nick has 189 trading cards. Kyle has 198 trading cards. Who has fewer cards?

   _____

3. A piano has 36 black keys and 52 white keys. Are there more black keys or white keys on a piano?

   _____

4. There are 253 cookies in a bag. There are 266 cookies in a box. Are there fewer cookies in the bag or in the box?

   _____

© Houghton Mifflin Harcourt Publishing Company

Lesson Check (2.NBT.4)

1. Gina has 245 stickers. Circle the number less than 245.

285   254

245   239

2. Carl's book has 176 pages. Circle the number greater than 176.

203   174

168   139

Spiral Review (2.NBT.1, 2.NBT.3)

3. Write 63 as a sum of tens and ones.

_____ + _____

4. Write the number 58 in tens and ones.

_____ tens _____ ones

5. Mr. Ford drove 483 miles during his trip. How many hundreds are in this number?

_____

6. Write 20 in words.

_____

Algebra • Compare Numbers

COMMON CORE STANDARD—2.NBT.4
Understand place value.

Compare the numbers. Write >, <, or =.

1. 489
605

489 ◯ 605

2. 719
719

719 ◯ 719

3. 370
248

370 ◯ 248

4. 645
654

645 ◯ 654

5. 205
250

205 ◯ 250

6. 813
781

813 ◯ 781

7. 397
393

397 ◯ 393

8. 504
405

504 ◯ 405

Problem Solving

Solve. Write or draw to explain.

9. Toby has 178 pennies.
Bella has 190 pennies.
Who has more pennies?

_____ has more pennies.

Lesson Check (2.NBT.4)

1. Write >, <, or = to compare.

315 ◯ 351

2. Write >, <, or = to compare.

401 ◯ 399

Spiral Review (2.OA.3, 2.NBT.1, 2.NBT.1a, 2.NBT.1b, 2.NBT.2)

3. What number has the same value as 50 tens?

_____

4. Write a number with an 8 in the hundreds place.

_____

5. Ned counts by fives. He starts at 80. Which number should he say next?

_____

6. Mr. Dean has an even number of cats and an odd number of dogs. Show how many dogs and cats he might have.

6 cats and _____ dogs

Dear Family,

My class started Chapter 3 this week. In this chapter, we will use different ways to practice our basic addition and subtraction facts.

Love, _____

Vocabulary

addend 4 + 5 = 9
The addends are **4** and **5**.

sum 4 + 5 = 9
The sum is **9**.

difference 12 − 4 = 8
The difference is **8**.

Home Activity

Write 5 addition problems (with sums through 10) on individual slips of paper. Write their sums on separate slips. Have your child choose a sum and then match it to the correct addition problem. Repeat until all the problems have been matched correctly with sums.

Literature

Reading math stories reinforces ideas. Look for these books at the library.

Cats Add Up
by Marilyn Burns and Dianne Ochiltree.
Cartwheel Books, 1998.

Each Orange Had 8 Slices
by Paul Giganti.
HarperTrophy, 1999.

Carta
para la casa

Querida familia:

Mi clase comenzó el Capítulo 3 esta semana. En este capítulo, usaremos diferentes modos de practicar nuestras operaciones básicas de suma y resta.

Con cariño, _____

Vocabulario

sumando $4 + 5 = 9$
Los sumandos son **4** y **5**.

suma $4 + 5 = 9$
La suma es **9**.

diferencia $12 - 4 = 8$
La diferencia es **8**.

Actividad para la casa

Escriba 5 problemas de suma (con sumas hasta 10) en diferentes pedazos de papel. Escriba los totales en papeles diferentes. Pídale a su hijo que elija un total y lo haga coincidir con el problema correcto. Repita los pasos hasta que todos los problemas concuerden con los totales.

Literatura

Leer cuentos de matemáticas refuerza los conceptos. Busque estos libros en la biblioteca.

Cats Add Up
por Marilyn Burns y Dianne Ochiltree. Cartwheel Books, 1998.

Each Orange Had 8 Slices
por Paul Giganti. HarperTrophy, 1999.

Practice Addition Facts

COMMON CORE STANDARD—2.OA.2
Add and subtract within 20.

Write the sums.

1. $9 + 1 = $ ____

   $1 + 9 = $ ____

2. $7 + 6 = $ ____

   $6 + 7 = $ ____

3. $8 + 0 = $ ____

   $5 + 0 = $ ____

4. ____ $= 7 + 9$

   ____ $= 9 + 7$

5. $4 + 4 = $ ____

   $4 + 5 = $ ____

6. $9 + 9 = $ ____

   $9 + 8 = $ ____

7. $8 + 8 = $ ____

   $8 + 7 = $ ____

8. $2 + 2 = $ ____

   $2 + 3 = $ ____

9. ____ $= 6 + 3$

   ____ $= 3 + 6$

10. $6 + 6 = $ ____

    $6 + 7 = $ ____

11. ____ $= 0 + 7$

    ____ $= 0 + 9$

12. $5 + 5 = $ ____

    $5 + 6 = $ ____

13. $8 + 5 = $ ____

    $5 + 8 = $ ____

14. $8 + 2 = $ ____

    $2 + 8 = $ ____

15. $7 + 4 = $ ____

    $4 + 7 = $ ____

Problem Solving

Solve. Write or draw to explain.

16. Jason has 7 puzzles. Quincy has the same number of puzzles as Jason. How many puzzles do they have altogether?

_____ puzzles

Lesson Check (2.OA.2)

1. What is the sum?

$$8 + 7 = \underline{\hphantom{000}}$$

2. What is the sum?

$$2 + 9 = \underline{\hphantom{000}}$$

Spiral Review (2.NBT.2, 2.NBT.3, 2.NBT.4, 2.NBT.8)

3. Write another way to describe 43.

$$\underline{\hphantom{000}} + \underline{\hphantom{000}}$$

4. Write the number that is 100 more than 276.

$$\underline{\hphantom{000}}$$

5. Count by tens.

20, 30, 40, \underline{\hphantom{00}}, \underline{\hphantom{00}}, \underline{\hphantom{00}}

6. Write <, >, or = to compare.

127 \underline{\hphantom{00}} 142

Algebra • Make a Ten to Add

COMMON CORE STANDARD—2.OA.2
Add and subtract within 20.

Show how you can make a ten to find the sum.
Write the sum.

1. $9 + 7 =$ ____

      1   6

   $10 +$ ____ $=$ ____

2. $8 + 5 =$ ____

   $10 +$ ____ $=$ ____

3. $8 + 6 =$ ____

   $10 +$ ____ $=$ ____

4. $3 + 9 =$ ____

   $10 +$ ____ $=$ ____

5. $8 + 7 =$ ____

   $10 +$ ____ $=$ ____

6. $6 + 5 =$ ____

   $10 +$ ____ $=$ ____

7. $7 + 6 =$ ____

   $10 +$ ____ $=$ ____

8. $5 + 9 =$ ____

   $10 +$ ____ $=$ ____

Problem Solving (Real World)

Solve. Write or draw to explain.

9. There are 9 children on the bus. Then 8 more children get on the bus. How many children are on the bus now?

_____ children

Lesson Check (2.OA.2)

1. Circle the fact with the same sum as 8 + 7.

10 + 3

10 + 4

10 + 5

10 + 6

2. Write a fact with the same sum as 7 + 5.

_____ + _____

Spiral Review (2.OA.3, 2.NBT.3)

3. Write the number shown by 200 + 10 + 7?

_____

4. Circle the odd number.

2   4   6   7

5. What is the value of the underlined digit?

6̲5

_____

6. What is another way to write the number 47?

_____ tens _____ ones

Algebra • Add 3 Addends

COMMON CORE STANDARD—2.OA.2
Add and subtract within 20.

Solve two ways. Circle the two addends you add first.

1. $2 + 3 + 7 =$ _____ $2 + 3 + 7 =$ _____

2. $5 + 3 + 3 =$ _____ $5 + 3 + 3 =$ _____

3. $4 + 5 + 4 =$ _____ $4 + 5 + 4 =$ _____

4. $4 + 4 + 4 =$ _____ $4 + 4 + 4 =$ _____

5.
$$\begin{array}{r} 5 \\ 4 \\ + 5 \\ \hline \end{array} \qquad \begin{array}{r} 5 \\ 4 \\ + 5 \\ \hline \end{array}$$

6.
$$\begin{array}{r} 6 \\ 3 \\ + 4 \\ \hline \end{array} \qquad \begin{array}{r} 6 \\ 3 \\ + 4 \\ \hline \end{array}$$

Problem Solving

Choose a way to solve. Write or draw to explain.

7. Amber has 2 red crayons, 5 blue crayons, and 4 yellow crayons. How many crayons does she have?

_____ crayons

Lesson Check (2.OA.2)

1. What is the sum of
2 + 4 + 6?

_____

2. What is the sum of
5 + 4 + 2?

_____

Spiral Review (2.NBT.1a, 2.NBT.1b, 2.NBT.3, 2.NBT.4, 2.NBT.8)

3. Write >, <, or = to compare.

688 _____ 648

4. What number can be written
as 4 tens 2 ones?

_____

5. What number has the same
value as 50 tens?

_____

6. What is the next number in
the pattern?

420, 520, 620, 720, _____

Algebra • Relate Addition and Subtraction

COMMON CORE STANDARD—2.OA.2
Add and subtract within 20.

Write the sum and the difference for the related facts.

1. $9 + 6 =$ ____

   $15 - 6 =$ ____

2. $8 + 5 =$ ____

   $13 - 5 =$ ____

3. $9 + 9 =$ ____

   $18 - 9 =$ ____

4. $7 + 3 =$ ____

   $10 - 3 =$ ____

5. $7 + 5 =$ ____

   $12 - 5 =$ ____

6. $6 + 8 =$ ____

   $14 - 6 =$ ____

7. $6 + 7 =$ ____

   $13 - 6 =$ ____

8. $8 + 8 =$ ____

   $16 - 8 =$ ____

9. $6 + 4 =$ ____

   $10 - 4 =$ ____

10. $7 + 9 =$ ____

    $16 - 9 =$ ____

11. $9 + 4 =$ ____

    $13 - 9 =$ ____

12. $8 + 7 =$ ____

    $15 - 7 =$ ____

Problem Solving Real World

Solve. Write or draw to explain.

13. There are 13 children on the bus. Then
    5 children get off the bus. How many
    children are on the bus now?

    ____ children

Lesson Check (2.OA.2)

1. Write a related addition fact for $15 - 6 = 9$.

   ___ + ___ = ___

2. Write a related subtraction fact for $5 + 7 = 12$.

   ___ − ___ = ___

Spiral Review (2.NBT.1, 2.NBT.3, 2.NBT.8)

3. What is another way to write 4 hundreds?

   ___

4. What is the next number in the pattern?

   515, 615, 715, 815, ___

5. What number is 10 more than 237?

   ___

6. Write the number 110 as a sum of hundreds and tens.

   ___ + ___

Practice Subtraction Facts

COMMON CORE STANDARD—2.OA.2
Add and subtract within 20.

Write the difference.

1. $15 - 9 =$ _____

2. $10 - 2 =$ _____

3. _____ $= 13 - 5$

4. $14 - 7 =$ _____

5. $10 - 8 =$ _____

6. $12 - 7 =$ _____

7. _____ $= 10 - 3$

8. $16 - 7 =$ _____

9. $8 - 4 =$ _____

10. $11 - 5 =$ _____

11. $13 - 6 =$ _____

12. _____ $= 12 - 9$

13. $16 - 9 =$ _____

14. _____ $= 11 - 9$

15. $12 - 8 =$ _____

16. $14 - 8 =$ _____

17. $10 - 5 =$ _____

18. $12 - 5 =$ _____

19. $15 - 7 =$ _____

20. $14 - 9 =$ _____

21. $17 - 9 =$ _____

Problem Solving

Solve. Write or draw to explain.

22. Mr. Li has 16 pencils. He gives 9 pencils to some students. How many pencils does Mr. Li have now?

_____ pencils

Lesson Check (2.OA.2)

1. Write the difference.

$$13 - 6 = \underline{\hspace{1cm}}$$

2. Write the difference.

$$12 - 3 = \underline{\hspace{1cm}}$$

Spiral Review (2.NBT.1, 2.NBT.1a, 2.NBT.1b, 2.NBT.2, 2.NBT.3)

3. What is the value of the underlined digit?

6<u>2</u>5

____

4. Count by fives.

405, ____, ____, ____

5. Devin has 39 toy blocks. What is the value of the digit 9 in this number?

____

6. Which number has the same value as 20 tens?

____

Use Ten to Subtract

COMMON CORE STANDARD—2.OA.2
Add and subtract within 20.

Show the tens fact you used.
Write the difference.

1. $14 - 6 =$ _____

   $10 -$ _____ $=$ _____

2. $12 - 7 =$ _____

   $10 -$ _____ $=$ _____

3. $13 - 7 =$ _____

   $10 -$ _____ $=$ _____

4. $15 - 8 =$ _____

   $10 -$ _____ $=$ _____

5. $11 - 7 =$ _____

   $10 -$ _____ $=$ _____

6. $14 - 5 =$ _____

   $10 -$ _____ $=$ _____

Problem Solving · Real World

Solve. Write or draw to explain.

7. Carl read 15 pages on Monday night and
   9 pages on Tuesday night. How many more
   pages did he read on Monday night than on
   Tuesday night?

   _____ more pages

Lesson Check (2.OA.2)

1. Show the tens fact you used.
   Write the difference.

   $12 - 6 =$ _____
   $10 - 4 =$ _____

2. Show the tens fact you used.
   Write the difference.

   $13 - 8 =$ _____
   $10 - 5 =$ _____

Spiral Review (2.OA.2, 2.NBT.4)

3. Write a related subtraction
   fact for $7 + 3 = 10$.

   _____

4. Joe has 8 trucks. Carmen has
   1 more truck than Joe. How
   many trucks do they have
   together?

   _____

5. There were 276 people on
   an airplane. Write a number
   greater than 276.

   _____

6. Write $>$, $<$, or $=$ to compare.

   537 _____ 375

Algebra • Use Drawings to Represent Problems

 COMMON CORE STANDARD—2.OA.1
Represent and solve problems involving addition and subtraction.

Complete the bar model. Then write a number sentence to solve.

1. Sara has 4 yellow beads and 3 green beads. How many beads does Sara have?

_____

____ beads

2. Adam had 12 trucks. He gave 4 trucks to Ed. How many trucks does Adam have now?

_____

____ trucks

3. Grandma has 14 red roses and 7 pink roses. How many more red roses than pink roses does she have?

_____

_____ more red roses

Lesson Check (2.OA.1)

1. Abby has 16 grapes. Jason has 9 grapes. How many more grapes does Abby have than Jason?

16
9

Spiral Review (2.OA.2, 2.NBT.3)

2. Write a subtraction fact with the same difference as $16 - 7$.

_____

3. What is the difference?

$$18 - 9 = \underline{\quad}$$

4. What is another way to write $300 + 20 + 5$?

_____

5. What is the value of the underlined digit?

2̲8

Algebra • Use Equations to Represent Problems

COMMON CORE STANDARD—2.OA.1
Represent and solve problems involving addition and subtraction.

Write a number sentence for the problem.
Use a ▇ for the unknown number. Then solve.

1. There were 15 apples in a bowl.
   Dan used some apples to make
   a pie. Now there are 7 apples in
   the bowl. How many apples did
   Dan use?

   _____

   _____ apples

2. Amy has 16 gift bags. She fills
   8 gift bags with whistles. How
   many gift bags are not filled
   with whistles?

   _____

   _____ gift bags

3. There were 5 dogs at the park.
   Then 9 more dogs joined them.
   How many dogs are at the
   park now?

   _____

   _____ dogs

Problem Solving

Write or draw to show
how you solved the problem.

4. Tony has 7 blue cubes and 6 red cubes.
   How many cubes does he have?

   _____ cubes

Lesson Check (2.OA.1)

1. Fred peeled 9 carrots. Nancy peeled 6 carrots. How many fewer carrots did Nancy peel than Fred?

_____

2. Omar has 8 marbles. Joy has 7 marbles. How many marbles do they have together?

_____

Spiral Review (2.OA.2, 2.NBT.1)

3. What is the sum?

$$8 + 8 = \_\_\_\_$$

4. What is the sum?

$$5 + 4 + 3 = \_\_\_\_$$

5. What has the same value as 1 hundred 7 tens?

_____

6. Which of the following is a way to describe the number 358?

_____ hundreds _____ tens _____ ones

Problem Solving • Equal Groups

COMMON CORE STANDARD—2.OA.4
Work with equal groups of objects to gain foundations for multiplication.

**Act out the problem.
Draw to show what you did.**

1. Mr. Anderson has 4 plates of cookies. There are 5 cookies on each plate. How many cookies are there?

_____ cookies

2. Ms. Trane puts some stickers in 3 rows. There are 2 stickers in each row. How many stickers does Ms. Trane have?

_____ stickers

3. There are 5 books in each box. How many books are in 5 boxes?

_____ books

Lesson Check (2.OA.4)

1. Jaime puts 3 oranges on each tray. How many oranges are on 5 trays?

_____

2. Maurice has 4 rows of toys with 4 toys in each row. How many toys does he have?

_____

Spiral Review (2.OA.1, 2.OA.2, 2.OA.3)

3. Jack has 12 pencils and 7 pens. How many more pencils than pens does he have?

_____ pencils

4. Laura has 9 apples. Jon has 6 apples. How many apples do they have together?

_____ apples

5. Circle the even number.

I   3   5   8

6. What is the sum?

$7 + 9 =$ _____

Algebra • Repeated Addition

COMMON CORE STANDARD—2.OA.4
Work with equal groups of objects to gain
foundations for multiplication.

Find the number of shapes in each row.
Complete the addition sentence to find
the total.

1.

3 rows of _____

_____ + _____ + _____ = _____

2.

2 rows of _____

_____ + _____ = _____

3.

4 rows of _____

_____ + _____ + _____ + _____ = _____

4.

4 rows of _____

_____ + _____ + _____ + _____ = _____

Problem Solving

Solve. Write or draw to explain.

5. A classroom has 3 rows of desks.
There are 5 desks in each row. How
many desks are there altogether?

_____ desks

Lesson Check

1. A scrapbook has 4 pages. There are 2 stickers on each page. How many stickers are there?

_____ stickers

2. Ben makes 5 rows of coins. He puts 3 coins in each row. How many coins are there?

_____ coins

Spiral Review (2.OA.2, 2.NBT.2, 2.NBT.3)

3. There are 5 apples and 4 oranges. How many pieces of fruit are there?

_____ pieces

4. Count by tens.

40, _____, _____, _____, _____

5. Write the number 260 using words.

_____

6. Write a fact with the same sum as 7 + 5.

_____

School-Home Letter

Dear Family,

My class started Chapter 4 this week. In this chapter, I will learn how to solve addition problems with 2-digit addends using different strategies.

Love, _____

Vocabulary

regroup To make a group of 10 ones and trade it for a ten

Home Activity

Pretend you are going on a treasure hunt. Using small pieces of paper, make a path in a small area. Each piece of paper should have an addition problem on it for your child to solve. At the end of the path, place a treasure of some kind.

Literature

Reading math stories reinforces ideas. Look for these books at the library.

A Collection for Kate by Barbara deRubertis. Kane Press, 1999.

Mission: Addition by Loreen Leedy. Holiday House, 1997.

Carta
para la **casa**

Querida familia:

Mi clase comenzó el Capítulo 4 esta semana. En este capítulo, aprenderé a resolver problemas con sumandos de dos dígitos usando diferentes estrategias.

Con cariño, _____

Vocabulario

reagrupar formar un grupo de 10 unidades y cambiarlo por en una decena

Actividad para la casa

Jueguen a buscar un tesoro. Con pequeños trozos de papel, haga un camino en un espacio pequeño. Cada trozo de papel deberá tener un problema para que su hijo lo resuelva. Al final del camino, coloque algún tipo de tesoro.

Literatura

Leer cuentos de matemáticas refuerza los conceptos. Busque estos libros en la biblioteca.

A Collection for Kate por Barbara deRubertis. Kane Press, 1999.

Mission: Addition por Loreen Leedy. Holiday House, 1997.

Break Apart Ones to Add

COMMON CORE STANDARD—2.NBT.6
Use place value understanding and properties
of operations to add and subtract.

**Break apart ones to make a ten.
Then add and write the sum.**

1. $62 + 9 =$ _____	2. $27 + 7 =$ _____
3. $28 + 5 =$ _____	4. $17 + 8 =$ _____
5. $57 + 6 =$ _____	6. $23 + 9 =$ _____
7. $39 + 7 =$ _____	8. $26 + 5 =$ _____
9. $13 + 8 =$ _____	10. $18 + 7 =$ _____
11. $49 + 8 =$ _____	12. $27 + 5 =$ _____
13. $39 + 4 =$ _____	14. $18 + 8 =$ _____

Problem Solving Real World

Solve. Write or draw to explain.

15. Jimmy had 18 toy airplanes. His mother
bought him 7 more toy airplanes. How many
toy airplanes does he have now?

_____ toy airplanes

Lesson Check (2.NBT.6)

I. What is the sum?

$$26 + 7 = \underline{\hspace{1cm}}$$

2. What is the sum?

$$15 + 8 = \underline{\hspace{1cm}}$$

Spiral Review (2.OA.1, 2.OA.2, 2.NBT.3)

3. Hannah has 4 blue beads and 8 red beads. How many beads does Hannah have?

$$4 + 8 = \underline{\hspace{1cm}} \text{ beads}$$

4. Rick had 4 stickers. Then he earned 2 more. How many stickers does he have now?

$$4 + 2 = \underline{\hspace{1cm}} \text{ stickers}$$

5. What is the sum?

$$4 + 5 + 4 = \underline{\hspace{1cm}}$$

6. Write 281 using hundreds, tens, and ones.

____ hundreds ____ tens ____ one

Use Compensation

COMMON CORE STANDARD—2.NBT.6
Use place value understanding and properties of operations to add and subtract.

Show how to make one addend the next
tens number. Complete the new addition sentence.

1. 15 + 37 = ?   ____ + ____ = ____

2. 22 + 49 = ?   ____ + ____ = ____

3. 38 + 26 = ?   ____ + ____ = ____

4. 27 + 47 = ?   ____ + ____ = ____

Problem Solving

Solve. Write or draw to explain.

5. The oak tree at the school was 34 feet tall.
   Then it grew 18 feet taller.
   How tall is the oak tree now?

   _____ feet tall

Lesson Check (2.NBT.6)

1. What is the sum?

$$18 + 25 = \underline{\hspace{1cm}}$$

2. What is the sum?

$$27 + 24 = \underline{\hspace{1cm}}$$

Spiral Review (2.OA.2, 2.OA.3)

3. Circle the even number.

27   14   11   5

4. Andrew sees 4 fish. Kim sees double that number of fish. How many fish does Kim see?

____ fish

5. Write is a related subtraction fact for $7 + 6 = 13$.

_____

6. What is the sum?

$$2 + 8 = \underline{\hspace{1cm}}$$

Name _____

Break Apart Addends as Tens and Ones

COMMON CORE STANDARD—2.NBT.6
Use place value understanding and properties of operations to add and subtract.

Break apart the addends to find the sum.

1. 18 ⟶ ___ + ___
    + 21 ⟶ ___ + ___

    ___ + ___ = ___

2. 33 ⟶ ___ + ___
    + 49 ⟶ ___ + ___

    ___ + ___ = ___

3. 72 ⟶ ___ + ___
    + 18 ⟶ ___ + ___

    ___ + ___ = ___

Problem Solving

Choose a way to solve.
Write or draw to explain.

4. Christopher has 28 baseball cards.
   Justin has 18 baseball cards. How
   many baseball cards do they
   have together?

   _____ baseball cards

Lesson Check (2.NBT.6)

1. What is the sum?

$$\begin{array}{r} 27 \\ + 12 \\ \hline \end{array}$$

2. What is the sum?

$$\begin{array}{r} 17 \\ + 35 \\ \hline \end{array}$$

Spiral Review (2.OA.2, 2.NBT.1, 2.NBT.3, 2.NBT.6)

3. What is the value of the underlined digit?

2<u>5</u>

_____

4. What number has the same value as 12 tens?

_____

5. Ally has 7 connecting cubes. Greg has 4 connecting cubes. How many connecting cubes do they have?

_____ cubes

6. Juan painted a picture of a tree. First he painted 15 leaves. Then he painted 23 more leaves. How many leaves did he paint?

_____ leaves

Model Regrouping for Addition

COMMON CORE STANDARDS—2.NBT.6
Use place value understanding and properties of operations to add and subtract.

Draw to show the regrouping. Write how many tens and ones in the sum. Write the sum.

1. Add 63 and 9.

Tens	Ones

_____ tens _____ ones

_____

2. Add 25 and 58.

Tens	Ones

_____ tens _____ ones

_____

3. Add 58 and 18.

Tens	Ones

_____ tens _____ ones

_____

4. Add 64 and 26.

Tens	Ones

_____ tens _____ ones

_____

5. Add 17 and 77.

Tens	Ones

_____ tens _____ ones

_____

6. Add 16 and 39.

Tens	Ones

_____ tens _____ ones

_____

Problem Solving

Choose a way to solve.
Write or draw to explain.

7. Cathy has 43 leaves in her collection.
Jane has 38 leaves. How many leaves
do the two children have?

_____ leaves

Lesson Check (2.NBT.6)

1. Add 27 and 48. What is the sum?

Tens	Ones

___

Spiral Review (2.OA.2, 2.OA.3, 2.NBT.6)

2. What is the sum?

$$7 + 7 = \underline{\quad}$$

3. Circle the odd number.

6   12   21   22

4. What is the sum?

$$39 + 46 = \underline{\quad}$$

5. What is the sum?

$$5 + 3 + 4 = \underline{\quad}$$

Model and Record 2-Digit Addition

COMMON CORE STANDARD—2.NBT.6
Use place value understanding and properties of operations to add and subtract.

Draw quick pictures to help you solve.
Write the sum.

1.

Tens	Ones
☐ 3	8
+ 1	7

Tens	Ones

2.

Tens	Ones
☐ 5	8
+ 2	6

Tens	Ones

3.

Tens	Ones
☐ 4	2
+ 3	7

Tens	Ones

4.

Tens	Ones
☐ 5	3
+ 3	8

Tens	Ones

Problem Solving

Choose a way to solve.
Write or draw to explain.

5. There were 37 children at the park on
Saturday and 25 children at the park
on Sunday. How many children were
at the park on those two days?

_____ children

Lesson Check (2.NBT.6)

1. What is the sum?

Tens	Ones
☐	
3	4
+ 2	8

2. What is the sum?

Tens	Ones
☐	
4	3
+ 2	7

Spiral Review (2.OA.2)

3. Adam collected 14 pennies in the first week and 9 pennies in the second week. How many more pennies did he collect in the first week than in the second week?

14 − 9 = _____ pennies

4. What is the sum?

3 + 7 + 9 = _____

5. Janet has 5 marbles. She finds double that number of marbles in her art box. How many marbles does Janet have now?

5 + _____ = _____ marbles

6. What is the difference?

13 − 5 = _____

2-Digit Addition

COMMON CORE STANDARD—2.NBT.5
*Use place value understanding and properties
of operations to add and subtract.*

Regroup if you need to. Write the sum.

1.
```
  4 │ 7
+ 2 │ 5
```

2.
```
  3 │ 3
+ 1 │ 8
```

3.
```
  2 │ 8
+ 6 │ 4
```

4.
```
  1 │ 3
+ 6 │ 5
```

5.
```
  1 │ 7
+ 2 │ 6
```

6.
```
  3 │ 6
+ 5 │ 3
```

7.
```
  5 │ 8
+ 2 │ 5
```

8.
```
  3 │ 7
+ 4 │ 9
```

9.
```
  5 │ 2
+ 2 │ 9
```

10.
```
  6 │ 6
+ 2 │ 4
```

11.
```
  7 │ 4
+ 1 │ 4
```

12.
```
  3 │ 7
+ 3 │ 7
```

Problem Solving

Solve. Write or draw to explain.

13. Angela drew 16 flowers on her paper in the morning. She drew 25 more flowers in the afternoon. How many flowers did she draw?

_____ flowers

Lesson Check (2.NBT.5)

1. What is the sum?

$$\begin{array}{r} 2\ |\ 1 \\ +\ 3\ |\ 7 \\ \hline \end{array}$$

2. What is the sum?

$$\begin{array}{r} 3\ |\ 8 \\ +\ 5\ |\ 2 \\ \hline \end{array}$$

Spiral Review (2.OA.1, 2.NBT.3, 2.NBT.8)

3. What is the next number in the counting pattern?

103, 203, 303, 403, _____

4. Rita counted 13 bubbles. Ben counted 5 bubbles. How many fewer bubbles did Ben count than Rita?

13 − 5 = _____ bubbles

5. Which number is 100 more than 265?

_____

6. Write 42 as a sum of tens and ones.

_____ + _____

Practice 2-Digit Addition

COMMON CORE STANDARD—2.NBT.5
Use place value understanding and properties
of operations to add and subtract.

Write the sum.

1.
```
   58
 + 17
```

2.
```
   44
 + 86
```

3.
```
   36
 + 13
```

4.
```
   49
 + 72
```

5.
```
   58
 + 87
```

6.
```
   32
 + 59
```

7.
```
   77
 + 58
```

8.
```
   45
 + 45
```

9.
```
   54
 + 28
```

Problem Solving

Solve. Write or draw to explain.

10. There are 45 books on the shelf.
There are 37 books on the table.
How many books are on the shelf
and the table?

_____ books

Lesson Check (2.NBT.5)

1. What is the sum?

$$56 + 35$$

2. What is the sum?

$$74 + 15$$

Spiral Review (2.OA.1, 2.OA.2, 2.NBT.1, 2.NBT.3)

3. What is the value of the underlined digit?

$\underline{5}26$

_____

4. Mr. Stevens wants to put 17 books on the shelf. He put 8 books on the shelf. How many more books does he need to put on the shelf?

$17 - 8 =$ _____ books

5. What is the difference?

$11 - 6 =$ _____

6. Write 83 as a sum of tens and ones.

_____ + _____

Rewrite 2-Digit Addition

COMMON CORE STANDARD—2.NBT.5
Use place value understanding and properties
of operations to add and subtract

Rewrite the numbers. Then add.

1. 27 + 19	2. 36 + 23	3. 31 + 29	4. 48 + 23
+ _____	+ _____	+ _____	+ _____
5. 53 + 12	6. 69 + 13	7. 24 + 38	8. 46 + 37
+ _____	+ _____	+ _____	+ _____

Problem Solving

Use the table. Show how you solved the problem.

9. How many pages did Sasha and Kara read together?

_____ pages

Pages Read This Week	
Child	**Number of Pages**
Sasha	62
Kara	29
Juan	50

Lesson Check (2.NBT.5)

1. What is the sum of 39 + 17?

$$+ \underline{}$$

2. What is the sum of 28 + 16?

$$+ \underline{}$$

Spiral Review (2.OA.4, 2.NBT.1, 2.NBT.3, 2.NBT.6)

3. What number is another way to write 60 + 4?

_____

4. The classroom has 4 desks in each row. There are 5 rows. How many desks are there in the classroom?

_____ desks

5. A squirrel collected 17 acorns. Then the squirrel collected 31 acorns. How many acorns did the squirrel collect?

_____ acorns

6. What number can be written as 3 hundreds 7 tens 5 ones?

_____

Problem Solving • Addition

COMMON CORE STANDARD—2.OA.1
Represent and solve problems involving addition and subtraction.

Label the bar model. Write a number sentence with a ▪ for the missing number. Solve.

1. Jacob counts 37 ants on the sidewalk and 11 ants on the grass. How many ants does Jacob count?

   _____

   _____ ants

2. There are 14 bees in the hive and 17 bees in the garden. How many bees are there?

   _____

   _____ bees

3. There are 28 flowers in Sasha's garden. 16 flowers are yellow and the rest are white. How many white flowers are in Sasha's garden?

   _____

   _____ white flowers

Lesson Check (2.OA.1)

1. Sean and Abby have 23 markers altogether. Abby has 14 markers. How many markers does Sean have?

_____

2. Mrs. James has 22 students in her class. Mr. Williams has 24 students in his class. How many students are in the two classes?

_____

Spiral Review (2.OA.2, 2.NBT.8)

3. What is the difference?

$$15 - 9 = \underline{\hphantom{00}}$$

4. What is the sum?

$$7 + 5 = \underline{\hphantom{00}}$$

5. Jan has 14 blocks. She gives 9 blocks to Tim. How many blocks does Jan have now?

$$14 - 9 = \underline{\hphantom{00}} \text{ blocks}$$

6. What is the next number in the counting pattern?

29, 39, 49, 59, _____

Algebra • Write Equations to Represent Addition

COMMON CORE STANDARD—2.OA.1
Represent and solve problems involving addition and subtraction.

Write a number sentence for the problem.
Use a ▓ for the missing number. Then solve.

1. Emily and her friends went to the park. They saw 15 robins and 9 blue jays. How many birds did they see?

_____

_____ birds

2. Joe has 13 fish in one tank. He has 8 fish in another tank. How many fish does Joe have?

_____

_____ fish

Problem Solving

Solve.

3. There are 21 children in Kathleen's class. 12 of the children are girls. How many children in her class are boys?

_____ boys

Lesson Check

1. Clare has 14 blocks. Jasmine has 6 blocks. How many blocks do they have?

$14 + 6 =$ _____ blocks

2. Matt finds 16 acorns at the park. Trevor finds 18 acorns. How many acorns do they find?

$16 + 18 =$ _____ acorns

Spiral Review (2.OA.1, 2.OA.2, 2.OA.3, 2.OA.4)

3. Leanne counted 19 ants. Gregory counted 6 ants. How many more ants did Leanne count than Gregory?

$19 - 6 =$ _____ ants

4. What is the sum?

$4 + 3 + 6 =$ _____

5. Ms. Santos puts seashells into 4 rows. She puts 6 seashells in each row. How many seashells are there altogether?

_____ seashells

6. Circle the even number.

9   14   17   21

P92 ninety-two

© Houghton Mifflin Harcourt Publishing Company

Algebra • Find Sums for 3 Addends

COMMON CORE STANDARD—2.NBT.6
Use place value understanding and properties of operations to add and subtract.

Add.

1.
```
  2 3
  2 0
+ 2 5
```

2.
```
  1 5
  2 2
+ 3 8
```

3.
```
  1 3
  5 2
+ 3 4
```

4.
```
  2 7
  4 0
+ 1 9
```

5.
```
  3 1
  4 5
+ 2 4
```

6.
```
  3 4
  1 1
+ 2 8
```

7.
```
  4 2
  3 6
+ 1 1
```

8.
```
  1 8
  2 2
+ 3 4
```

9.
```
  5 3
  1 9
+ 2 5
```

Problem Solving

Solve. Write or draw to explain.

10. Liam has 24 yellow pencils, 15 red pencils, and 9 blue pencils. How many pencils does he have altogether?

_____ pencils

Lesson Check (2.NBT.6)

1. What is the sum?

$$
\begin{array}{r}
22 \\
31 \\
+\ 16 \\
\hline
\end{array}
$$

2. What is the sum?

$$
\begin{array}{r}
17 \\
26 \\
+\ 30 \\
\hline
\end{array}
$$

Spiral Review (2.OA.1, 2.OA.4, 2.NBT.3, 2.NBT.8)

3. What number is 10 more than 127?

_____

4. Mr. Howard's phone has 4 rows of buttons. There are 3 buttons in each row. How many buttons are on Mr. Howard's phone?

_____ buttons

5. Bob tosses 8 horseshoes. Liz tosses 9 horseshoes. How many horseshoes do they toss?

$8 + 9 =$ _____ horseshoes

6. What number can be written 3 hundreds 1 ten 5 ones?

_____

Algebra • Find Sums for 4 Addends

COMMON CORE STANDARD—2.NBT.6
Use place value understanding and properties of operations to add and subtract.

Add.

1.
```
  1 8
  3 2
  2 3
+   3
```

2.
```
  4 5
  3 1
  2 9
+ 7 2
```

3.
```
  2 4
  6 2
  7 0
+ 3 3
```

4.
```
  8 3
  3 2
  6 1
+ 2 2
```

5.
```
  3 7
  1 5
  3 1
+ 1 2
```

6.
```
  2 1
  1 3
  9 6
+ 1 8
```

Problem Solving Real World

Solve. Show how you solved the problem.

7. Kinza jogs 16 minutes on Monday, 13 minutes on Tuesday, 9 minutes on Wednesday, and 20 minutes on Thursday. What is the total number of minutes she jogged?

_____ minutes

Lesson Check (2.NBT.6)

1. What is the sum?

$$
\begin{array}{r}
1\,2 \\
3\,3 \\
5\,6 \\
+\,3\,2 \\
\hline
\end{array}
$$

2. What is the sum?

$$
\begin{array}{r}
4\,1 \\
7\,4 \\
4\,3 \\
+\,2\,0 \\
\hline
\end{array}
$$

Spiral Review (2.OA.1, 2.NBT.5)

3. Laura had 6 daisies. Then she found 7 more daisies. How many daisies does she have now?

$6 + 7 =$ _____ daisies

4. What is the sum?

$$
\begin{array}{r}
5\,2 \\
+\,2\,7 \\
\hline
\end{array}
$$

5. Alan has 25 trading cards. He buys 8 more. How many cards does he have now?

$25 + 8 =$ _____ cards

6. Jen saw 13 guinea pigs and 18 gerbils at the pet store. How many pets did she see?

$13 + 18 =$ _____ pets

Dear Family,

My class started Chapter 5 this week. In this chapter, I will learn how to solve 2-digit subtraction problems using different strategies.

Love, _____

Vocabulary

minus sign a symbol used in a subtraction problem

difference the answer to a subtraction problem

$$7 - 4 = 3$$

↑
difference

Home Activity

Write 2-digit numbers, such as 56, 67, and 89, each on a separate index card. Use a pencil and a paper clip to make a pointer for the spinner. Have your child choose a card, spin the pointer, and subtract the number on the spinner from the number on the card.

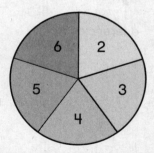

Literature

Look for these books at the library. Read them with your child to reinforce learning.

The Action of Subtraction
by Brian P. Cleary
Millbrook Press, 2006

The Shark Swimathon
by Stuart J. Murphy
HarperCollins, 2001

Carta
para la casa

Querida familia:

Mi clase comenzó el Capítulo 5 esta semana. En este capítulo, aprenderé a resolver problemas de resta de números de 2 dígitos usando estrategias diferentes.

Con cariño, _____

Vocabulario

signo de menos símbolo que se usa en un problema de resta

diferencia la respuesta a un problema de resta

$$7 - 4 = 3$$

↑
diferencia

Actividad para la casa

Escriba números de 2 dígitos, como 56, 67 y 89, cada uno en una tarjeta. Con un lápiz y un clip, haga una flecha giratoria para la rueda. Pida a su hijo que elija una tarjeta, gire la flecha, y reste el número en que se detenga en la rueda del número de la tarjeta.

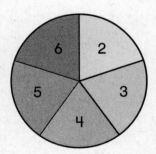

Literatura

Busque estos libros en la biblioteca. Léalos con su hijo para reforzar el aprendizaje.

The Action of Subtraction
por Brian P. Cleary
Millbrook Press, 2006

The Shark Swimathon
por Stuart J. Murphy
HarperCollins, 2001

Name _____

Algebra • Break Apart Ones to Subtract

COMMON CORE STANDARD—2.NBT.5
Use place value understanding and properties of operations to add and subtract.

**Break apart ones to subtract.
Write the difference.**

1. 36 − 7 = _____

2. 35 − 8 = _____

3. 37 − 9 = _____

4. 41 − 6 = _____

5. 44 − 5 = _____

6. 33 − 7 = _____

7. 32 − 4 = _____

8. 31 − 6 = _____

9. 46 − 9 = _____

10. 43 − 5 = _____

Problem Solving

Choose a way to solve. Write or draw to explain.

11. Beth had 44 marbles. She gave
9 marbles to her brother.
How many marbles does
Beth have now?

_____ marbles

Lesson Check (2.NBT.5)

1. What is the difference?

40 41 42 43 44 45 46 47 48 49 **50** 51 52 53 54 55 56 57 58 59 **60** 61 62 63 64 65 66 67 68 69 **70**

$$58 - 9 = \underline{}$$

Spiral Review (2.OA.2, 2.NBT.6)

2. What is the difference?

$$14 - 6 = \underline{}$$

3. What is the sum?

$$3 + 6 + 2 = \underline{}$$

4. What is the sum?

$$64 + 7 = \underline{}$$

5. What is the sum?

$$56 + 18 = \underline{}$$

Algebra • Break Apart Numbers to Subtract

COMMON CORE STANDARD—2.NBT.5
Use place value understanding and properties
of operations to add and subtract.

Break apart the number you are subtracting. Write the difference.

1. $81 - 14 =$ _____

2. $84 - 16 =$ _____

3. $77 - 14 =$ _____

4. $83 - 19 =$ _____

5. $81 - 17 =$ _____

6. $88 - 13 =$ _____

7. $84 - 19 =$ _____

8. $86 - 18 =$ _____

9. $84 - 17 =$ _____

10. $76 - 15 =$ _____

11. $86 - 12 =$ _____

12. $82 - 19 =$ _____

Problem Solving

Solve. Write or draw to explain.

13. Mr. Pearce bought 43 plants. He gave
14 plants to his sister. How many
plants does Mr. Pearce have now?

_____ plants

Lesson Check (2.NBT.5)

1. What is the difference?

$$63 - 19 = \underline{\hspace{1cm}}$$

Spiral Review (2.OA.1, 2.OA.2, 2.NBT.6)

2. What is the sum?

$$\begin{array}{r} 14 \\ + 23 \\ \hline \end{array}$$

3. What is the sum?

$$8 + 7 = \underline{\hspace{1cm}}$$

4. Write a related subtraction fact for $6 + 8 = 14$.

_____

5. John has 7 kites. Annie has 4 kites. How many kites do they have altogether?

____ kites

Model Regrouping for Subtraction

COMMON CORE STANDARDS—2.NBT.5
Use place value understanding and properties of operations to add and subtract.

Draw to show the regrouping.
Write the difference two ways.
Write the tens and ones. Write the number.

1. Subtract 9 from 35.

Tens	Ones

_____ tens _____ ones

_____

2. Subtract 14 from 52.

Tens	Ones

_____ tens _____ ones

_____

3. Subtract 17 from 46.

Tens	Ones

_____ tens _____ ones

_____

4. Subtract 28 from 63.

Tens	Ones

_____ tens _____ ones

_____

Problem Solving

Choose a way to solve. Write or draw to explain.

5. Mr. Ortega made 51 cookies. He gave 14 cookies away. How many cookies does he have now?

_____ cookies

Lesson Check (2.NBT.9, 2.NBT.5)

1. Subtract 9 from 36.
What is the difference?

Tens	Ones

———

2. Subtract 28 from 45.
What is the difference?

Tens	Ones

———

Spiral Review (2NBT.5, 2.NBT.6)

3. What is the difference?

$$51 - 8 = \underline{\hspace{1cm}}$$

40 41 42 43 44 45 46 47 48 49 **50** 51 52 53 54 55 56 57 58 59 **60**

4. What is the sum?

$$38 + 35 = \underline{\hspace{1cm}}$$

5. What is the sum?

$$\begin{array}{r} 63 \\ 18 \\ + 9 \\ \hline \end{array}$$

Model and Record 2-Digit Subtraction

COMMON CORE STANDARD—2.NBT.5
Use place value understanding and properties of operations to add and subtract.

Draw a quick picture to solve.
Write the difference.

1.

Tens	Ones
□	□
4	3
− 1	7

Tens	Ones

2.

Tens	Ones
□	□
3	8
− 2	9

Tens	Ones

3.

Tens	Ones
□	□
5	2
− 3	7

Tens	Ones

4.

Tens	Ones
□	□
3	5
− 1	9

Tens	Ones

Problem Solving

Solve. Write or draw to explain.

5. Kendall has 63 stickers.
Her sister has 57 stickers.
How many more stickers does
Kendall have than her sister?

_____ more stickers

Lesson Check (2.NBT.5)

1. What is the difference?

Tens	Ones
4	7
− 1	8

2. What is the difference?

Tens	Ones
3	3
− 2	9

Spiral Review (2.OA.2, 2.NBT.5, 2.NBT.6)

3. What is the difference?

$$10 - 6 = \underline{}$$

4. What is the sum?

$$16 + 49 = \underline{}$$

5. What is the sum?

$$28 + 8 = \underline{}$$

6. What is the difference?

$$52 - 6 = \underline{}$$

2-Digit Subtraction

COMMON CORE STANDARD—2.NBT.5
Use place value understanding and properties
of operations to add and subtract.

Regroup if you need to.
Write the difference.

1.

Tens	Ones
☐	☐
4	7
− 2	8

2.

Tens	Ones
☐	☐
3	3
− 1	8

3.

Tens	Ones
☐	☐
2	8
− 1	4

4.

Tens	Ones
☐	☐
6	6
− 1	9

5.

```
  7   7
− 2   6
```

6.

```
  5   8
− 3   4
```

7.

```
  5   2
− 2   5
```

8.

```
  8   7
− 4   9
```

Problem Solving

Solve. Write or draw to explain.

9. Mrs. Paul bought 32 erasers. She gave
   19 erasers to students. How many erasers
   does she still have?

_____ erasers

Lesson Check (2.NBT.5)

1. What is the difference?

$$
\begin{array}{r}
4\ |\ 8 \\
-\ 3\ |\ 9 \\
\hline
\end{array}
$$

2. What is the difference?

$$
\begin{array}{r}
8\ |\ 4 \\
-\ 6\ |\ 6 \\
\hline
\end{array}
$$

Spiral Review (2.OA.1, 2.OA.2, 2.NBT.5)

3. What is the difference?

Tens	Ones
3	2
− 1	9

4. Write an addition fact that will give the same sum as 8 + 7.

$$10 + \underline{\quad}$$

5. 27 boys and 23 girls go on a field trip to the museum. How many children go to the museum?

_____ children

6. There were 17 berries in the basket. Then 9 berries are eaten. How many berries are there now?

_____ berries

Practice 2-Digit Subtraction

COMMON CORE STANDARD—2.NBT.5
*Use place value understanding and properties
of operations to add and subtract.*

Write the difference.

1.
$$
\begin{array}{r}
5\ 0 \\
-1\ 8 \\
\hline
\end{array}
$$

2.
$$
\begin{array}{r}
4\ 3 \\
-1\ 7 \\
\hline
\end{array}
$$

3.
$$
\begin{array}{r}
7\ 5 \\
-1\ 8 \\
\hline
\end{array}
$$

4.
$$
\begin{array}{r}
2\ 2 \\
-\ \ 6 \\
\hline
\end{array}
$$

5.
$$
\begin{array}{r}
6\ 0 \\
-3\ 5 \\
\hline
\end{array}
$$

6.
$$
\begin{array}{r}
4\ 2 \\
-3\ 4 \\
\hline
\end{array}
$$

7.
$$
\begin{array}{r}
2\ 1 \\
-\ \ 8 \\
\hline
\end{array}
$$

8.
$$
\begin{array}{r}
3\ 9 \\
-2\ 7 \\
\hline
\end{array}
$$

9.
$$
\begin{array}{r}
6\ 1 \\
-3\ 7 \\
\hline
\end{array}
$$

Problem Solving

Solve. Write or draw to explain.

10. Julie has 42 sheets of paper.
She gives 17 sheets to Kari.
How many sheets of paper
does Julie have now?

_____ sheets of paper

Lesson Check (2.NBT.5)

1. What is the difference?

$$\begin{array}{r} 73 \\ -\ 47 \\ \hline \end{array}$$

2. What is the difference?

$$\begin{array}{r} 54 \\ -\ 13 \\ \hline \end{array}$$

Spiral Review (2.OA.2, 2.NBT.6)

3. What is the sum?

$9 + 9 =$ _____

4. What is the difference?

$14 - 7 =$ _____

5. What is the sum?

$36 + 25 =$ _____

6. What is the sum?

$7 + 2 + 3 =$ _____

Rewrite 2-Digit Subtraction

COMMON CORE STANDARD—2.NBT.5
Use place value understanding and properties
of operations to add and subtract.

**Rewrite the subtraction problem.
Then find the difference.**

1. $35 - 19$

2. $47 - 23$

3. $55 - 28$

___ ___
‾‾‾‾‾‾‾‾‾   ‾‾‾‾‾‾‾‾‾   ‾‾‾‾‾‾‾‾‾

4. $22 - 15$

5. $61 - 32$

6. $70 - 37$

___ ___ ___
‾‾‾‾‾‾‾‾‾   ‾‾‾‾‾‾‾‾‾   ‾‾‾‾‾‾‾‾‾

Problem Solving

Solve. Write or draw to explain.

7. Jimmy went to the toy store. He saw
23 wooden trains and 41 plastic trains.
How many more plastic trains than
wooden trains did he see?

_____ more plastic trains

Lesson Check (2.NBT.5)

1. What is the difference for
43 − 17?

_____ −
_____

2. What is the difference for
50 − 16?

_____ −
_____

Spiral Review (2.OA.2, 2.NBT.5, 2.NBT.6, 2.NBT.9)

3. What is the sum?

$$
\begin{array}{r}
29 \\
4 \\
25 \\
+\ 16 \\
\hline
\end{array}
$$

4. What is the sum of 41 + 19?

_____

5. Write an addition fact that will
give the same sum as 5 + 9?

10 + ___

6. What is the difference?

45 − 13 = ___

Add to Find Differences

COMMON CORE STANDARD—2.NBT.5
Use place value understanding and properties of operations to add and subtract.

Use the number line. Count up to find the difference.

1. 36 − 29 = ____

20 21 22 23 24 25 26 27 28 29 **30** 31 32 33 34 35 36 37 38 39 **40**

2. 43 − 38 = ____

30 31 32 33 34 35 36 37 38 39 **40** 41 42 43 44 45 46 47 48 49 **50**

3. 76 − 68 = ____

60 61 62 63 64 65 66 67 68 69 **70** 71 72 73 74 75 76 77 78 79 **80**

Problem Solving

Solve. You may wish to use the number line.

50 51 52 53 54 55 56 57 58 59 **60** 61 62 63 64 65 66 67 68 69 **70**

4. Jill has 63 index cards. She uses 57 of them for a project. How many index cards does Jill have now?

____ index cards

Lesson Check (2.NBT.5)

Use the number line. Count up to find the difference.

70 71 72 73 74 75 76 77 78 79 **80** 81 82 83 84 85 86 87 88 89 **90**

1. 82 − 75 = _____

2. 90 − 82 = _____

Spiral Review (2.OA.1, 2.OA.4, 2.NBT.5, NBT.9)

3. Jordan has 41 toy cars at home. He brings 24 cars to school. How many cars are at home?

_____ cars

4. Pam has 15 fish. 9 are goldfish and the rest are guppies. How many fish are guppies?

_____ guppies

5. What is the sum?

```
  3 | 5
+ 1 | 9
```

6. Each table has 5 pencils. There are 3 tables. How many pencils are there altogether?

_____ pencils

Problem Solving • Subtraction

COMMON CORE STANDARD—2.OA.1
Represent and solve problems involving
addition and subtraction.

Label the bar model. Write a
number sentence with a ▨ for
the missing number. Solve.

1. Megan picked 34 flowers. Some
   of the flowers are yellow and
   18 flowers are pink. How many
   of the flowers are yellow?

_____ yellow flowers

_____

2. Alex had 45 toy cars. He put
   26 toy cars in a box. How many
   toy cars are not in the box?

_____ toy cars

_____

3. Mr. Kane makes 43 pizzas. 28
   of the pizzas are small. The rest
   are large. How many pizzas
   are large?

_____ large pizzas

_____

Lesson Check (2.OA.1)

1. There were 39 pumpkins at the store. Then 17 of the pumpkins were sold. How many pumpkins are still at the store?

   _____ pumpkins

2. There were 48 ants on a hill. Then 13 of the ants marched away. How many ants are still on the hill?

   _____ ants

Spiral Review (2.OA.1, 2.OA.2, 2.NBT.5, 2.NBT.6)

3. Ashley had 26 markers. Her friend gave her 17 more markers. How many markers does Ashley have now?

   _____ markers

4. What is the sum?

$$46 + 24$$

5. Write a subtraction fact that will give the same difference as 15 − 7.

   $10 - \underline{\quad}$

6. What is the sum?

   $34 + 5 = \underline{\quad}$

Algebra • Write Equations to Represent Subtraction

COMMON CORE STANDARD—2.OA.1
Represent and solve problems involving addition and subtraction.

**Write a number sentence for the problem.
Use a ▇ for the missing number. Then solve.**

I. 29 children rode their bikes
to school. After some of the
children rode home, there were
8 children with bikes still at
school. How many children
rode their bikes home?

_____

_____ children

2. 32 children were on the school
bus. Then 24 children got off
the bus. How many children were
still on the bus?

_____

_____ children

Problem Solving Real World

Solve. Write or draw to explain.

3. There were 21 children in the library.
After 7 children left the library, how many
children were still in the library?

_____ children

Lesson Check (2.OA.1)

1. Cindy had 42 beads. She used some beads for a bracelet. She has 14 beads left. How many beads did she use for the bracelet?

_____ beads

2. Jake had 36 baseball cards. He gave 17 cards to his sister. How many baseball cards does Jake have now?

_____ cards

Spiral Review (2.OA.2, 2.NBT.5)

3. What is the sum?

$6 + 7 =$ _____

4. What is the difference?

$16 - 9 =$ _____

5. What is the difference?

$$\begin{array}{r} 4\,6 \\ -\ 3\,9 \\ \hline \end{array}$$

6. Write an addition fact that will give the same sum as $6 + 8$.

$10 +$ _____

Solve Multistep Problems

 COMMON CORE STANDARD—2.OA.1
Represent and solve problems involving addition and subtraction.

Complete the bar models for the steps you do to solve the problem.

1. Greg has 60 building blocks. His sister gives him 17 more blocks. He uses 38 blocks to make a tower. How many blocks are not used in the tower?

_____ blocks

2. Jenna has a train of 26 connecting cubes and a train of 37 connecting cubes. She gives 15 cubes to a friend. How many cubes does Jenna have now?

_____ cubes

Problem Solving

Solve. Write or draw to explain.

3. Ava has 25 books. She gives away 7 books. Then Tom gives her 12 books. How many books does Ava have now?

_____ books

Lesson Check (2.OA.1)

1. Sara has 18 crayons. Max has 19 crayons. How many more crayons do they need to have 50 crayons altogether?

_____ crayons

2. Jon has 12 pennies. Lucy has 17 pennies. How many more pennies do they need to have 75 pennies altogether?

_____ pennies

Spiral Review (2.OA.1, 2.NBT.5, 2.NBT.6)

3. What is the difference?

$$58 - 13 = \underline{\quad}$$

40 41 42 43 44 45 46 47 48 49 50 51 52 53 54 55 56 57 58 59 60

4. What is the sum?

$$\begin{array}{r} 4\ 7 \\ +\ 1\ 5 \\ \hline \end{array}$$

5. There are 26 cards in a box. Bryan takes 12 cards. How many cards are still in the box?

_____ cards

School-Home Letter

Dear Family,

My class started Chapter 6 this week. In this chapter, I will learn how to add and subtract 3-digit numbers, including regrouping ones, tens, and hundreds.

Love, _____

Vocabulary

addends Numbers added together in addition problems

$7 + 2 = 9$

addends

sum Answer to an addition problem

$7 + 2 = 9$

sum

difference Answer to a subtraction problem

Home Activity

Write addition and subtraction problems with two 3-digit numbers for your child. Write some problems where regrouping is needed and other problems where regrouping is not needed.

$$462 + 341$$ $$796 - 578$$

Literature

Reading math stories reinforces learning. Look for these books at the library.

A Collection for Kate by Barbara deRubertis. Kane Press, 1999.

The Action of Subtraction by Brian P. Cleary. Millbrook Press, 2006.

Carta
para la casa

Querida familia:

Mi clase comenzó el Capítulo 6 esta semana. En este capítulo, aprenderé a sumar y restar números de 3 dígitos, incluyendo la reagrupación de unidades, decenas y centenas.

Con cariño, _____

Vocabulario

sumandos números que se suman unos a otros en problemas de suma

$$7 + 2 = 9$$
sumandos

suma resultado de un problema de suma

$$7 + 2 = 9$$
suma

diferencia resultado de un problema de resta

Actividad para la casa

Escríbale a su hijo problemas de suma y resta con dos números de 3 dígitos. Escriba algunos problemas que necesiten reagrupación y otros que no la necesiten.

$$462 \atop +341$$

$$796 \atop -578$$

Literatura

Leer cuentos de matemáticas refuerza el aprendizaje. Busque estos libros en la biblioteca.

A Collection for Kate por Barbara Derubertis. Kane Press, 1999.

The Action of Subtraction por Brian P. Cleary. Millbrook Press, 2006.

Draw to Represent 3-Digit Addition

 COMMON CORE STANDARD—2.NBT.7
Use place value understanding and properties of operations to add and subtract.

Draw quick pictures. Write how many hundreds, tens, and ones in all. Write the number.

1. Add 142 and 215.

Hundreds	Tens	Ones

$$\begin{array}{r} 142 \\ +215 \\ \hline 357 \end{array}$$

__3__ hundreds __5__ tens __7__ ones

__357__

2. Add 263 and 206.

Hundreds	Tens	Ones

____ hundreds ____ tens ____ ones

_____

 Problem Solving · Real World

Solve. Write or draw to explain.

3. A farmer sold 324 lemons and 255 limes. How many pieces of fruit did the farmer sell altogether?

_____ pieces of fruit

Lesson Check (2.NBT.7)

1. Ms. Carol sold 346 child tickets and 253 adult tickets. How many tickets did Ms. Carol sell?

_____ tickets

2. Mr. Harris counted 227 gray pebbles and 341 white pebbles. How many pebbles did Mr. Harris count?

_____ pebbles

Spiral Review (2.OA.4, 2.NBT.5, 2.NBT.6)

3. Pat has 3 rows of shells. There are 4 shells in each row. How many shells does Pat have?

_____ shells

4. Kara counted 32 red pens, 25 blue pens, 7 black pens, and 24 green pens. How many pens did Kara count?

_____ pens

5. Kai had 46 blocks. He gave 39 blocks to his sister. How many blocks does Kai have left?

$46 - 39 =$ _____ blocks

6. A shop has 55 posters for sale. 34 posters show sports. The rest of the posters show animals. How many posters show animals?

_____ posters

Break Apart 3-Digit Addends

COMMON CORE STANDARD—2.NBT.7
Use place value understanding and properties of operations to add and subtract.

Break apart the addends to find the sum.

1. $\begin{array}{r} 518 \\ + 221 \end{array}$ → _____ + _____ + _____

   → _____ + _____ + _____

   _____ + _____ + _____ = _____

2. $\begin{array}{r} 438 \\ + 142 \end{array}$ → _____ + _____ + _____

   → _____ + _____ + _____

   _____ + _____ + _____ = _____

3. $\begin{array}{r} 324 \\ + 239 \end{array}$ → _____ + _____ + _____

   → _____ + _____ + _____

   _____ + _____ + _____ = _____

Problem Solving

Solve. Write or draw to explain.

4. There are 126 crayons in a bucket. A teacher puts 144 more crayons in the bucket. How many crayons are in the bucket now?

   _____ crayons

Lesson Check (2.NBT.7)

1. What is the sum?

$$\begin{array}{r} 218 \\ + 145 \\ \hline \end{array}$$

2. What is the sum?

$$\begin{array}{r} 664 \\ + 223 \\ \hline \end{array}$$

Spiral Review (2.OA.2, 2.NBT.5, 2.NBT.6, 2.NBT.9)

3. Ang found 19 berries and Barry found 21 berries. How many berries did they find altogether?

$$19 + 21 = \text{\_\_\_\_ berries}$$

4. Write a subtraction fact related to $9 + 6 =$

_____

5. There are 25 goldfish and 33 betta fish. How many fish are there?

$$25 + 33 = \text{\_\_\_\_ fish}$$

6. Subtract 16 from 41. What is the difference?

Tens	Ones

3-Digit Addition: Regroup Ones

COMMON CORE STANDARD—2.NBT.7
Use place value understanding and properties
of operations to add and subtract.

Write the sum.

1.

Hundreds	Tens	Ones
	☐	
1	4	8
+ 2	3	4

2.

Hundreds	Tens	Ones
	☐	
3	2	1
+ 3	1	8

3.

Hundreds	Tens	Ones
	☐	
4	1	4
+ 1	7	9

4.

Hundreds	Tens	Ones
	☐	
6	0	2
+ 2	5	8

Problem Solving `Real World`

Solve. Write or draw to explain.

5. In the garden, there are 258 yellow
daisies and 135 white daisies. How many
daisies are in the garden altogether?

_____ daisies

Lesson Check (2.NBT.7)

1. What is the sum?

Hundreds	Tens	Ones
	□	
4	3	5
+ 1	4	6

2. What is the sum?

Hundreds	Tens	Ones
	□	
4	3	6
+ 3	0	6

Spiral Review (2.OA.2, 2.NBT.5, 2.NBT.6, 2.NBT.7)

3. What is the difference?

$$9 - 4 = \underline{\hspace{1cm}}$$

4. What is the sum?

$$\begin{array}{r} 82 \\ + 59 \\ \hline \end{array}$$

5. What is the sum?

$$26 + 7 = \underline{\hspace{1cm}}$$

6. Add 243 and 132. How many hundreds, tens, and ones are there in all?

____ hundreds ____ tens

____ ones

3-Digit Addition: Regroup Tens

COMMON CORE STANDARD—2.NBT.7
Use place value understanding and properties of operations to add and subtract.

Write the sum.

1.

Hundreds	Tens	Ones
☐	☐	
1	8	7
+ 2	3	2

2.

Hundreds	Tens	Ones
☐	☐	
3	2	2
+ 3	5	6

3.

Hundreds	Tens	Ones
☐	☐	
2	8	5
+ 5	3	1

4.

4	4	5
+	3	4

5.

6	2	0
+ 2	8	8

6.

5	5	7
+ 1	8	0

7.

```
   6 7 1
 + 1 5 4
```

8.

```
   4 6 3
 + 4 8 1
```

9.

```
   7 4 6
 + 1 3 3
```

Problem Solving

Solve. Write or draw to explain.

10. There are 142 blue toy cars and
293 red toy cars at the toy store.
How many toy cars are there?

_____ toy cars

Lesson Check (2.NBT.7)

1. What is the sum?

$$472 + 255$$

2. Annika has 144 pennies and Yahola has 284 pennies. How many do they have altogether?

$$144 + 284$$

Spiral Review (2.OA.2, 2.NBT.5, 2.NBT.7)

3. What is the sum?

$$56 + 38$$

4. What is the sum?

$$326 + 139$$

5. Francis had 8 toy cars, then his brother gave him 9 more. How many toy cars does Francis have now?

$8 + 9 =$ _____ cars

6. What is the difference?

$$82 - 34$$

Addition: Regroup Ones and Tens

COMMON CORE STANDARD—2.NBT.7
Use place value understanding and properties
of operations to add and subtract.

Write the sum.

1.
```
  5 4 7
+ 4 3 5
```

2.
```
  3 6 7
+ 2 8 4
```

3.
```
  4 8 5
+ 4 5 6
```

4.
```
  1 8 7
+ 3 0 6
```

5.
```
  6 4 7
+ 1 2 8
```

6.
```
  5 2 3
+ 1 7 4
```

7.
```
  2 5 5
+ 2 3 1
```

8.
```
  2 9 4
+ 1 7 6
```

9.
```
  3 7 5
+ 3 6 4
```

Problem Solving

Solve. Write or draw to explain.

10. Saul and Luisa each scored 167 points
    on a computer game. How many points
    did they score together?

_____ points

Lesson Check (2.NBT.7)

1. What is the sum?

$$348 \\ + \ 272$$

2. What is the sum?

$$123 \\ + \ 217$$

Spiral Review (2.OA.1, 2.OA.2, 2.NBT.6, 2.NBT.9)

3. Which addition fact has the same sum as $9 + 4$.

$$10 + \underline{\hspace{1cm}}$$

4. What is the sum?

$$32 \\ 15 \\ + \ 46$$

5. Add 29 and 35. What is the sum?

Tens	Ones

$$\underline{\hspace{1.5cm}}$$

6. Tom had 25 pretzels. He gave away 12 pretzels. How many pretzels does Tom have left?

$$25 - 12 = \underline{\hspace{1cm}} \text{ pretzels}$$

Problem Solving • 3-Digit Subtraction

 COMMON CORE STANDARD—2.NBT.7
Use place value understanding and properties of operations to add and subtract.

Make a model to solve. Then draw a quick picture of your model.

1. On Saturday, 770 people went to the snack shop. On Sunday, 628 people went. How many more people went to the snack shop on Saturday than on Sunday?

_____ more people

2. There were 395 lemon ice cups at the snack shop. People bought 177 lemon ice cups. How many lemon ice cups are still at the snack shop?

_____ cups

3. There were 576 bottles of water at the snack shop. People bought 469 bottles of water. How many bottles of water are at the snack shop now?

_____ bottles

4. There were 279 bags of apple chips at the snack shop. Then 134 bags of apple chips were bought. How many bags of apple chips are at the snack shop now?

_____ bags

Lesson Check (2.NBT.7)

1. There are 278 math and science books. 128 of them are math books. How many science books are there?

_____ books

2. A book has 176 pages. Mr. Roberts has read 119 pages. How many pages does he have left to read?

_____ pages

Spiral Review (2.OA.2, 2.NBT.5, 2.NBT.6, 2.NBT.7)

3. What is the sum?

$$1 + 6 + 2 = \_\_\_$$

4. What is the difference?

$$54 - 8 = \_\_\_$$

5. What is the sum?

$$
\begin{array}{r}
356 \\
+\ 174 \\
\hline
\end{array}
$$

6. What is the sum?

$$
\begin{array}{r}
22 \\
+\ 16 \\
\hline
\end{array}
$$

3-Digit Subtraction: Regroup Tens

COMMON CORE STANDARD—2.NBT.7
Use place value understanding and properties
of operations to add and subtract.

Solve. Write the difference.

1.

Hundreds	Tens	Ones
	☐	☐
7	7	4
− 2	3	6

2.

Hundreds	Tens	Ones
	☐	☐
5	5	1
− 1	1	3

3.

Hundreds	Tens	Ones
	☐	☐
4	8	9
− 2	7	3

4.

Hundreds	Tens	Ones
	☐	☐
7	7	2
− 2	5	4

Problem Solving

Solve. Write or draw to explain.

5. There were 985 pencils. Some pencils
were sold. Then there were 559 pencils
left. How many pencils were sold?

_____ pencils

Lesson Check (2.NBT.7)

1. What is the difference?

$$346 - 127$$

2. What is the difference?

$$568 - 226$$

Spiral Review (2.OA.1, 2.OA.4, 2.NBT.5, 2.NBT.7)

3. What is the difference?

$$45 - 7 = \underline{}$$

4. Leroy has 11 cubes. Jane has 15 cubes. How many cubes do they have altogether?

_____ cubes

5. Mina puts 5 flowers in each vase. How many flowers will she put in 3 vases?

_____ flowers

6. Mr. Hill had 428 pencils. He gave away 150 pencils. How many pencils did he keep?

_____ pencils

3-Digit Subtraction: Regroup Hundreds

COMMON CORE STANDARD—2.NBT.7
Use place value understanding and properties of operations to add and subtract.

Solve. Write the difference.

1.

Hundreds	Tens	Ones
□	□	□
7	2	7
− 2	5	6

2.

Hundreds	Tens	Ones
□	□	□
9	6	7
− 1	5	3

3.

```
  6  3  9
− 4  7  2
```

4.

```
  4  4  8
− 3  6  3
```

Problem Solving Real World

Solve. Write or draw to explain.

5. There were 537 people in the parade. 254 of these people were playing an instrument. How many people were not playing an instrument?

_____ people

Lesson Check (2.NBT.7)

1. What is the difference?

$$\begin{array}{r} 538 \\ -135 \\ \hline \end{array}$$

2. What is the difference?

$$\begin{array}{r} 218 \\ -126 \\ \hline \end{array}$$

Spiral Review (2.OA.2, 2.NBT.5, 2.NBT.6, 2.NBT.7)

3. What is the difference?

$52 - 15 = \underline{}$

4. Wallace has 8 crayons and Alma has 7. How many do the have together?

$8 + 7 = \underline{}$ crayons

5. What is the sum?

$$\begin{array}{r} 47 \\ +26 \\ \hline \end{array}$$

6. Mrs. Lin's class read 392 books in February. Mr. Hook's class read 173 books. How many more books did Mrs. Lin's class read?

$$\begin{array}{r} 392 \\ -173 \\ \hline \end{array}$$

_____ books

Subtraction: Regroup Hundreds and Tens

COMMON CORE STANDARD—2.NBT.7
Use place value understanding and properties
of operations to add and subtract.

Solve. Write the difference.

1.
```
    8  1  6
  - 3  4  5
  _____
```

2.
```
    9  4  2
  - 1  6  3
  _____
```

3.
```
    7  9  6
  - 4  6  8
  _____
```

4.
```
    7  2  3
  - 5  4  3
  _____
```

5.
```
    9  8  6
  - 7  1  2
  _____
```

6.
```
    5  4  7
  - 2  8  9
  _____
```

Problem Solving

Solve.

7. Mia's coloring book has 432 pages. She has already colored 178 pages. How many pages in the book are left to color?

_____ pages

Lesson Check (2.NBT.7)

1. What is the difference?

$$\begin{array}{r} 349 \\ -\ 187 \\ \hline \end{array}$$

2. What is the difference?

$$\begin{array}{r} 336 \\ -\ 178 \\ \hline \end{array}$$

Spiral Review (2.OA.1, 2.OA.2, 2.NBT.5, 2.NBT.7)

3. What is the sum?

$$\begin{array}{r} 246 \\ +\ 533 \\ \hline \end{array}$$

4. What is the difference?

$$\begin{array}{r} 38 \\ -\ 14 \\ \hline \end{array}$$

5. What is the difference?

$17 - 9 = $ _____

6. Lisa had 15 daisies.
She gave away 7 daisies.
Then she found 3 more daisies.
How many daisies does Lisa
have now?

$15 - 7 + 3 = $ _____

Regrouping with Zeros

COMMON CORE STANDARD—2.NBT.7
Use place value understanding and properties
of operations to add and subtract.

Solve. Write the difference.

1.
```
   8 0 6
 - 3 4 5
```

2.
```
   9 0 2
 - 7 8 3
```

3.
```
   7 9 4
 - 2 6 8
```

4.
```
   6 8 7
 - 1 4 4
```

5.
```
   5 0 5
 - 1 6 7
```

6.
```
   3 0 7
 - 1 5 4
```

Problem Solving

Solve.

7. There are 303 students.
   There are 147 girls.
   How many boys are there?

_____ boys

Lesson Check (2.NBT.7)

1. What is the difference?

$$\begin{array}{r} 301 \\ -\ 187 \\ \hline \end{array}$$

2. What is the difference?

$$\begin{array}{r} 406 \\ -\ 268 \\ \hline \end{array}$$

Spiral Review (2.OA.2, 2.NBT.5, 2.NBT.7, 2.NBT.9)

3. What is the sum?

$$\begin{array}{r} 35 \\ +\ 79 \\ \hline \end{array}$$

4. There are 555 students at Roosevelt Elementary School and 282 students at Jefferson Elementary. How many students are at the two schools altogether?

$$\begin{array}{r} 555 \\ +\ 282 \\ \hline \end{array}$$

_____ students

5. What is the difference?

$$10 - 2 = \underline{\quad}$$

6. Gabriel's goal is to read 43 books this year. So far he has read 11 books. How many books does he have left to meet his goal?

$$\begin{array}{r} 43 \\ -\ 11 \\ \hline \end{array}$$

_____ books

Estimation in 3-Digit Subtraction

COMMON CORE STANDARD—2.NBT.7.1
Use estimation strategies with numbers up to 1,000.

Use the number lines to find the nearest hundred for each number. Then estimate the difference.

100   200   300   400   500   600

1.

$$\begin{array}{r} 390 \\ -\ 189 \\ \hline \end{array}$$

An estimate for the difference

is _____

$$\begin{array}{r} - \\ \hline \end{array}$$

2.

$$\begin{array}{r} 580 \\ -\ 139 \\ \hline \end{array}$$

An estimate for the difference

is _____

$$\begin{array}{r} - \\ \hline \end{array}$$

Problem Solving

Solve. Write or draw to explain.

3. Mike works at a paper mill. There are 790 employees at the mill in the daytime. There are 420 employees at the mill in the evening. Estimate how many more employees are at the mill in the daytime.

about _____ more employees

Lesson Check (2.NBT.7.1)

4. There are 490 people cheering for the Red team. There are 280 people cheering for the Blue team. Estimate about how many more people are cheering for the Red team.

about _____ more people

5. Estimate the difference.

$$\begin{array}{r} 740 \\ -\ 420 \\ \hline \end{array}$$

An estimate for the difference is _____

Spiral Review (2.NBT.7)

6. What is the difference?

$$\begin{array}{r} 605 \\ -\ 367 \\ \hline \end{array}$$

7. Janie picked 125 apples. Her brother picked 140 apples. How many apples did they pick altogether?

$$\begin{array}{r} 125 \\ +\ 140 \\ \hline \end{array}$$

8. What is the sum?

$$\begin{array}{r} 282 \\ +\ 405 \\ \hline \end{array}$$

9. Roger had 345 stickers. He gave his friend 120 stickers. How many stickers did he have left?

_____ stickers

School-Home
Letter

Dear Family,

My class started Chapter 7 this week. In this chapter, I will learn about the values of coins and how to find the total value of a group of money. I will also learn how to tell time on analog clocks and digital clocks.

Love, _____

Vocabulary

penny a coin with a value of 1 cent

nickel a coin with a value of 5 cents

dime a coin with a value of 10 cents

quarter a coin with a value of 25 cents

dollar an amount equal to 100 cents

minute a unit of time

Home Activity

With your child, set up a play store together. Use objects such as food items or small toys. Put price tags on each object, using amounts less than one dollar. On a sheet of paper, have your child write the price of an object and then draw a group of coins that has that as its total value. Take turns doing this for several objects.

Literature

Reading math stories reinforces ideas. Look for these books at the library.

A Dollar for Penny
by Julie Glass
Random House Books for Young Readers, 2000

What Time Is It, Mr. Crocodile?
by Judy Sierra
Gulliver Books, 2004

Carta para la casa

Querida familia:

Mi clase comenzó el Capítulo 7 esta semana. En este capítulo, aprenderé sobre el valor de las monedas y cómo hallar el valor total de una cantidad de dinero. También aprenderé a decir la hora usando relojes analógicos y relojes digitales.

Con cariño, _____

Vocabulario

moneda de 1¢ una moneda con un valor de 1 centavo

moneda de 5¢ una moneda con un valor de 5 centavos

moneda de 10¢ una moneda con valor de 10 centavos

moneda de 25¢ una moneda con valor de 25 centavos

dólar una cantidad igual a 100 centavos

minuto una unidad de tiempo

Actividad para la casa

Junto a su hijo, jueguen a que están en una tienda. Use objetos tales como artículos de comida o juguetes pequeños. Coloque etiquetas en cada artículo con un precio menor a un dólar. En una hoja de papel, pida su hijo que escriba el precio de un objeto y que dibuje un grupo de monedas que muestren ese valor. Túrnense para repetir la actividad con diferentes objetos.

Literatura

Leer cuentos de matemáticas refuerza los conceptos. Busque estos libros en la biblioteca.

A Dollar for Penny por Julie Glass. Random House Books for Young Readers, 2000.

What Time Is It, Mr. Crocodile? por Judy Sierra. Gulliver Books, 2004.

© Houghton Mifflin Harcourt Publishing Company

P148 one hundred forty-eight

Dimes, Nickels, and Pennies

COMMON CORE STANDARD—2.MD.8
Work with time and money.

Count on to find the total value.

1.

_____ total value

2.

_____ total value

3.

total value

4.

total value

Problem Solving Real World

Solve. Write or draw to explain.

5. Aaron has 5 dimes and 2 nickels.
   How much money does Aaron have?

_____

Lesson Check (2.MD.8)

1. What is the total value of this group of coins?

_____

Spiral Review (2.OA.2, 2.OA.4, 2.NBT.1, 2.NBT.2)

2. Hayden is building toy cars. Each car needs 4 wheels. How many wheels will Hayden use to build 3 toy cars?

_____ wheels

3. What is the value of the underlined digit?

4̲29

_____

4. Lillian is counting by fives. What numbers did she say next?

40, ____, ____, ____, ____

5. Sophie has 12 grapes in her lunch bag. She shared 7 grapes with her sister. How many grapes does she have?

12 − 7 = _____

Quarters

COMMON CORE STANDARD—2.MD.8
Work with time and money.

Count on to find the total value.

1.

_____

☐ total value

2.

_____

☐ total value

3.

☐ total value

Problem Solving Real World

Read the clue. Choose the name of a coin from the box to answer the question.

nickel	dime
quarter	penny

4. I have the same value as a group of 2 dimes and 1 nickel. What coin am I?

_____

Lesson Check (2.MD.8)

1. What is the total value of this group of coins?

_____

Spiral Review (2.OA.1, 2.OA.3, 2NBT.3, 2NBT.4)

2. Circle the odd number.

   8   14   17   22

3. Kai scored 4 points and Gail scored 7 points. How many points did they score altogether?

$4 + 7 =$ _____ points

---

4. There were 382 chairs in the music hall. Write a number greater than 382.

_____

5. Write the number 61 using words.

_____

Count Collections

COMMON CORE STANDARD—2.MD.8
Work with time and money.

Draw and label the coins from greatest to least value. Find the total value.

1.

_____

2.

_____

3.

_____

Problem Solving

Solve. Write or draw to explain.

4. Rebecca has these coins. She spends 1 quarter. How much money does she have left?

_____

Lesson Check (2.MD.8)

1. What is the total value of this group of coins?

_____

Spiral Review (2.OA.2, 2.NBT.1, 2.NBT.3, 2.NBT.8)

2. What number is 100 more than 562?

_____

3. Describe 58 as a sum of tens and ones.

_____

4. Pete helps his grandmother gather pecans. He finds 6 pecans on his left and 3 on his right. How many pecans did Pete find altogether?

6 + 3 = _____ pecans

5. What number do the blocks show?

_____

Show Amounts in Two Ways

COMMON CORE STANDARD—2.MD.8
Work with time and money.

Use coins. Show the amounts in two ways.
Draw and label the coins.

1.

   39¢

2.

   70¢

3.

   57¢

© Houghton Mifflin Harcourt

Problem Solving

4. Madeline uses fewer than 5 coins
   to pay 60¢. Draw coins to show
   one way she could pay 60¢.

Lesson Check (2.MD.8)

1. Circle the group of coins that has the same total value.

Spiral Review (2.OA.2, 2NBT.1, 2NBT.3)

2. Write the number 31 as a sum of tens and ones.

2 tens _____ ones

3. Write 13 tens as a sum of hundreds and tens.

_____ hundreds _____ tens

4. What is the value of the underlined digit?

2<u>8</u>

_____

5. Baylie's softball team scored 5 runs in the first inning and 6 runs in the second inning. How many runs did her team score?

5 + 6 = _____ runs

One Dollar

COMMON CORE STANDARD—2.MD.8
Work with time and money.

Circle coins to make $1.00.
Cross out the coins you do not use.

1.

2.

3.

Problem Solving Real World

4. Draw more coins to show $1.00 in all.

© Houghton Mifflin Harcourt Publishing Company

Lesson Check (2.MD.8)

1. Which group of coins has a value of $1.00?

Spiral Review (2.OA.3, 2.NBT.2, 2.NBT.3, 2.MD.8)

2. Write 692 using words.

_____

3. Keith ate 7 almonds, then ate 7 more. Is the total number of almonds even or odd?

7 + 7 = _____ almonds

_____

4. What is the total value of 1 quarter and 3 nickels?

_____

5. Kristin is counting by tens. What numbers does she say next?

230, _____,

_____, _____

Amounts Greater Than $1

COMMON CORE STANDARD—2.MD.8
Work with time and money.

Circle the money that makes $1.00. Then
write the total value of the money shown.

1.

_____

2.

_____

3.

_____

Problem Solving *Real World*

Solve. Write or draw to explain.

4. Grace found 3 quarters, 3 dimes,
and I nickel in her pocket. How
much money did she find?

_____

Lesson Check (2.MD.8)

1. Julie has this money in her bank. What is the total value of this money?

_____

Spiral Review (2.OA.2, 2.NBT.5, 2.NBT.8)

2. There are 79 squash plants and 42 pepper plants in Julia's garden. How many vegetable plants are in Julia's garden altogether?

```
    7 9
+   4 2
```

3. What is the difference?

```
    6 1
-   2 7
```

4. What number is 100 less than 694?

_____

5. Write an addition fact that has the same sum as 6 + 5.

10 + _____

Problem Solving • Money

COMMON CORE STANDARD—2.MD.8
Work with time and money.

Use play coins and bills to solve.
Draw to show what you did.

1. Sara has 2 quarters, 1 nickel, and two $1 bills.
   How much money does Sara have?   _____

2. Brad has one $1 bill, 4 dimes, and 2 nickels
   in his bank. How much money does Brad
   have in his bank?   _____

3. Mr. Morgan gives 1 quarter, 3 nickels, 4 pennies,
   and one $1 bill to the clerk. How much money
   does Mr. Morgan give the clerk?   _____

Lesson Check (2.MD.8)

1. Lee has two $1 bills and 4 dimes. How much money does Lee have?

_____

2. Dawn has 2 quarters, 1 nickel, and one $1 bill. How much money does Dawn have?

_____

Spiral Review (2.OA.2, 2.NBT.3, 2.NBT.4, 2.NBT.8)

3. What is the value of the underlined digit?

5<u>6</u>

____

4. Cecilia collected 342 pennies for her class's penny drive. Marked collected 243 pennies. Use <, >, or = to compare. Who collected more?

342 ____ 243

_____ collected more.

5. Brooke's dog has 15 treats. Then he ate 8 of them. How many treats does he have left?

15 − 8 = _____

6. What is the next number in this pattern?

225, 325, 425, 525, _____

Time to the Hour and Half Hour

COMMON CORE STANDARD—2.MD.7
Work with time and money.

Look at the clock hands. Write the time.

1.

2.

3.

4.

5.

6.

Problem Solving

7. Amy's music lesson begins at 4:00. Draw hands on the clock to show this time.

Lesson Check (2.MD.7)

1. What is the time on this clock?

_____

2. What is the time on this clock?

_____

Spiral Review (2.OA.3, 2.NBT.1, 2.NBT.4, 2.MD.8)

3. Rachel has one $1 bill, 3 quarters, and 2 pennies. How much money does Rachel have?

_____

4. Write <, >, or = to compare 260 and 362.

260 _____ 362

5. What number is shown with these blocks?

_____

6. Circle any even numbers.

1   3   4   5

Time to 5 Minutes

COMMON CORE STANDARD—2.MD.7
Work with time and money.

Look at the clock hands. Write the time.

1.

2.

3.

4.

5.

6.

Problem Solving Real World

Draw the minute hand to show the time. Then write the time.

7. My hour hand points between the 4 and the 5. My minute hand points to the 9. What time do I show?

© Houghton Mifflin Harcourt Publishing Company

Lesson Check (2.MD.7)

1. What is the time on this clock?

_____

2. What is the time on this clock?

_____

Spiral Review (2.OA.1, 2.OA.2, 2.OA.4, 2.NBT.1a, 2.NBT.1b)

3. What is the sum?

$1 + 6 + 8 =$ _____

4. Which number has the same value as 30 tens?

_____

5. Steven has 3 rows of toys. There are 4 toys in each row. How many toys are there?

_____ toys

6. Jill has 14 buttons. She buys 8 more buttons. How many buttons does Jill have?

$$\begin{array}{r} 14 \\ + 8 \\ \hline \end{array}$$

buttons

Practice Telling Time

COMMON CORE STANDARD—2.MD.7
Work with time and money.

Draw the minute hand to show the time. Write the time.

1. quarter past 7

2. half past 3

3. 50 minutes after 1

4. quarter past 11

5. 15 minutes after 8

6. 5 minutes after 6

Problem Solving

Draw hands on the clock to solve.

7. Josh got to school at half past 8.
Show this time on the clock.

Lesson Check (2.MD.7)

1. Write the time on this clock using words.

_____

Spiral Review (2.OA.4, 2.NBT.3, 2.MD.7, 2.MD.8)

2. What is the value of this group of coins?

_____

3. What time is shown on this clock?

_____

4. Write six hundred forty-seven using numbers.

_____

A.M. and P.M.

COMMON CORE STANDARD—2.MD.7
Work with time and money.

Write the time. Then circle A.M. or P.M.

1. walk the dog

A.M.

P.M.

2. finish breakfast

A.M.

P.M.

3. put on pajamas

A.M.

P.M.

4. read a bedtime story

A.M.

P.M.

Problem Solving Real World

Use the list of times. Complete the story.

5. Jess woke up at _____. She got on

the bus at _____ and went to school.

She left school at _____.

> 3:15 P.M.
> 8:30 A.M.
> 7:00 A.M.

Lesson Check (2.MD.7)

1. The clock shows when the soccer game ended. What time was it?

_____

2. The clock shows when Dad gets up for work. What time is it?

_____

Spiral Review (2.NBT.3, 2.NBT.7, 2.MD.7, 2.MD.8)

3. What coin has the same value as 25 pennies? Draw your answer.

4. Describe 72 as a sum of tens and ones.

_____ + _____

5. At the beginning of the school year there were 437 2nd graders at Woods Elementary. Over the course of the year, 24 students joined. How many 2nd graders are there at the end of the year?

$$\begin{array}{r} 437 \\ +24 \\ \hline \end{array}$$

_____ 2nd graders

6. What time is quarter past 3?

_____

Units of Time

COMMON CORE STANDARD—2.MD.7
Know relationships of time.

Use the calendars to answer the questions.

July

Sunday	Monday	Tuesday	Wednesday	Thursday	Friday	Saturday
		1	2	3	4	5
6	7	8	9	10	11	12
13	14	15	16	17	18	19
20	21	22	23	24	25	26
27	28	29	30	31		

September

Sunday	Monday	Tuesday	Wednesday	Thursday	Friday	Saturday
	1	2	3	4	5	6
7	8	9	10	11	12	13
14	15	16	17	18	19	20
21	22	23	24	25	26	27
28	29	30				

January

Sunday	Monday	Tuesday	Wednesday	Thursday	Friday	Saturday
			1	2	3	4
5	6	7	8	9	10	11
12	13	14	15	16	17	18
19	20	21	22	23	24	25
26	27	28	29	30	31	

1. List the months that each have greater than 30 days.

_____

_____

2. What is the date of the fifth Monday in September?

_____

_____

3. In July, there are 4 weeks and _____ days.

_____

4. Name an event that would be measured in days.

_____

Problem Solving

Solve. Write or draw to explain.

5. Cal's dog is 60 weeks old. Jin's dog is 1 year old. Which is the greater amount of time?

_____

Lesson Check (2.MD.7)

6. At the end of school, Omar was at home for 5 days. Then he went to camp for 1 week. Which is the greater amount of time?

_____

7. Rosie's cat stayed with Rosie's aunt for 40 days. It stayed with Rosie's grandma for 1 month. Which is the lesser amount of time?

_____

Spiral Review (2.NBT.7, 2.MD.8, 2.NBT.2, 2.NBT.7)

8. Ana's class sold 176 tickets to a show. There were 482 tickets for sale to begin. How many more tickets were there to sell?

_____ more tickets

9. Joe used 5 quarters and 4 dimes to pay for a pen. How much money did he use?

_____

10. Vicki used 5 buttons on each shirt. She made 3 shirts. Then she used 2 more buttons. How many buttons did Vicki use?

_____ buttons

11. On Friday, 294 children rode the fair ride. On Saturday, 358 children rode the fair ride. How many children rode the fair ride on the two days?

_____ children

Chapter 8

School-Home Letter

Dear Family,

My class started Chapter 8 this week. In this chapter, I will learn about inches and feet. I will also learn about measuring tools and showing measurement data.

Love, _____

Vocabulary

inch Unit of length

foot 12 inches

yardstick A tool that shows 3 feet

Home Activity

Record each family member's height with masking tape in a doorway of your house. Measure the height in inches. Write each person's name and height on the tape.

Literature

Reading math stories reinforces ideas. Look for these books at the library.

Measuring Penny by Loreen Leedy. Henry Holt and Company, 1998.

Twelve Snails to One Lizard by Susan Hightower. Simon & Schuster, 1997.

© Houghton Mifflin Harcourt Publishing Company

Capítulo 8

Carta para la casa

Querida familia:

Mi clase comenzó el Capítulo 8 esta semana. En este capítulo, aprenderé acerca de pulgadas y pies. También aprenderé sobre herramientas para medir y mostrar información sobre medidas.

Con cariño, _____

Vocabulario

pulgada Unidad de longitud

pulgadas

pie 12 pulgadas

regla de 1 yarda Una herramienta con marcas que mostra 3 pies

Actividad para la casa

En el marco de una puerta, marque con cinta adhesiva la altura de cada miembro de la familia. Mida la altura en pulgadas. Escriba el nombre de cada persona y su altura en la cinta adhesiva.

Literatura

La lectura de cuentos matemáticos refuerza las ideas. Busque estos libros en la biblioteca.

Measuring Penny por Loreen Leedy. Henry Holt and Company, 1998.

Twelve Snails to One Lizard por Susan Hightower. Simon & Schuster, 1997.

Estimate Lengths in Inches

COMMON CORE STANDARD—2.MD.3
Measure and estimate lengths in standard units.

The bead is 1 inch long.
Circle the best estimate for the length
of the string.

1.

   1 inch   4 inches   7 inches

2.

   3 inches   6 inches   9 inches

3.

   2 inches   3 inches   6 inches

4.

   2 inches   5 inches   8 inches

Problem Solving

Solve. Write or draw to explain.

5. Ashley has some beads. Each bead is
   2 inches long. How many beads will fit on
   a string that is 8 inches long?

   _____ beads

Lesson Check (2.MD.3)

1. The bead is 1 inch long. Estimate the length of the string.

_____ inches

Spiral Review (2.OA.1, 2.NBT.6, 2.MD.7)

2. Draw hands on the clock to show 5 minutes after 6.

3. Ella read 16 pages of her book on Monday and 26 pages on Tuesday. There are 64 pages in the book. How many more pages are left for Ella to read?

_____ pages

4. What is the sum?

38 + 24 = _____

Measure with an Inch Ruler

COMMON CORE STANDARD—2.MD.1
Measure and estimate lengths in standard units.

Measure the length to the nearest inch.

1.

_____ inches

2.

_____ inches

3.

_____ inches

4.

_____ inches

Problem Solving Real World

5. Measure the string. What is its total length?

_____ inches

Lesson Check (2.MD.1)

1. Use an inch ruler. What is the length to the nearest inch?

_____ inches

2. Use an inch ruler. What is the length to the nearest inch?

_____ inches

Spiral Review (2.OA.2, 2.MD.1, 2.MD.7)

3. The clock shows the time that Jen got to school. What time did Jen get to school?

_____ : _____ A.M.
          P.M.

4. What is the difference?

$$13 - 5 = \underline{\quad}$$

5. Each color tile is about 1 inch long. About how long is the ribbon?

about _____ inch / inches

Problem Solving • Add and Subtract in Inches

COMMON CORE STANDARDS—2.MD.5, 2.MD.6 *Relate addition and subtraction to length.*

Draw a diagram. Write a number sentence using a █ for the missing number. Solve.

1. Molly had a ribbon that was 23 inches long. She cut 7 inches off the ribbon. How long is her ribbon now?

_____

Molly's ribbon is _____ inches long now.

2. Jed has a paper clip chain that is 11 inches long. He adds 7 inches of paper clips to the chain. How long is the paper clip chain now?

_____

The paper clip chain is _____ inches long now.

Lesson Check (2.MD.5, 2.MD.6)

1. Allie has two pieces of string. Each one is 8 inches long. How many inches of string does she have altogether?

_____ inches

2. Jeff has a cube train that is 26 inches long. He removes 12 inches of cubes from the train. How long is Jeff's cube train now?

_____ inches

Spiral Review (2.MD.1, 2.MD.8)

3. Ann buys a pencil for 45 cents. Make a list of coins that would equal 45 cents.

_____

4. Use an inch ruler. About how long is the string?

about _____ inch

5. Jason has these coins in a jar. What is the total value of these coins?

$ _____ or _____ cents

Measure in Inches and Feet

COMMON CORE STANDARD—2.MD.2
Measure and estimate lengths in standard units.

Measure to the nearest inch.
Then measure to the nearest foot.

Find the real object.	Measure.
1. bookcase	_____ inches _____ feet
2. window	_____ inches _____ feet
3. chair	_____ inches _____ feet

Problem Solving Real World

4. Jake has a piece of yarn that is 4 feet long.
Blair has a piece of yarn that is 4 inches long.
Who has the longer piece of yarn? Explain.

_____

_____

Lesson Check (2.MD.2)

1. Larry is telling his sister about using a ruler to measure length. Fill in the blanks with 'inch' or 'foot' to make the sentence true.

I _____ is longer than I _____.

Spiral Review (2.NBT.5, 2.NBT.7, 2.MD.7, 2.MD.8)

2. Matt put this money in his pocket. What is the total value of this money?

$ _____

3. What time is shown on this clock?

___ : ___

4. Ali had 38 game cards. Her friend gave her 15 more game cards. How many game cards does Ali have now?

____ cards

Estimate Lengths in Feet

COMMON CORE STANDARD—2.MD.3
Measure and estimate lengths in standard units.

Find each object:
Estimate how many 12-inch rulers will
be about the same length as the object.

1. door

   Estimate: _____ rulers, or _____ feet

2. flag

   Estimate: _____ rulers, or _____ feet

3. wall of a small room

   Estimate: _____ rulers, or _____ feet

Problem Solving

Solve. Write or draw to explain.

4. Mr. and Mrs. Baker place 12-inch rulers along the length of a rug. They each line up 3 rulers along the edge of the rug. What is the length of the rug?

about _____ feet

Lesson Check (2.MD.3)

1. Estimate how many 12 inch rulers will be about the same length as a bike.

_____ rulers, or _____ feet

2. Estimate how many 12 inch rulers will be about the same length as a keyboard.

_____ rulers, or _____ feet

Spiral Review (2.NBT.5, 2.NBT.7, 2.MD.8)

3. What is the total value of 2 quarters, 3 dimes, and 4 nickels?

$ _____

4. What is the total value of 2 dimes, 3 nickels, and 2 pennies?

$ _____ or _____ cents

5. There are 68 children in the school. There are 19 children on the playground. How many more children are in the school than on the playground?

_____ children

6. What is the sum?

$$\begin{array}{r} 548 \\ + 436 \\ \hline \end{array}$$

Choose a Tool

COMMON CORE STANDARD—2.MD.1
Measure and estimate lengths in standard units.

Choose the best tool for measuring the real object. Then measure and record the length or distance.

inch ruler
yardstick
measuring tape

I. the length of your desk

Tool: _____

Length: _____

2. the distance around a basket

Tool: _____

Length: _____

Problem Solving

Choose the better tool for measuring.
Explain your choice.

3. Mark wants to measure the length of his room.
Should he use an inch ruler or a yardstick?

Mark should use _____ because

_____

_____

Lesson Check (2.MD.1)

1. Kim wants to measure the distance around her bike tire. Circle the best tool for her to use.

cup   yardstick

color tiles   measuring tape

2. Ben wants to measure the length of a seesaw. Circle the best tool for him to use.

cup   yardstick

color tiles   paper clips

Spiral Review (2.MD.2, 2.MD.3, 2.MD.5, 2.MD.6)

3. Estimate how many 12 inch rulers will be about the same length as a sheet of paper.

_____ ruler, or _____ foot

4. Andy has a rope that is 24 inches long. He cuts off 7 inches from the rope. How long is the rope now?

_____ inches

5. Jan is telling her friend about using a ruler to measure length. Fill in the blanks with inches or foot to make the sentence true.

12 _____ is the same length as 1 _____.

Display Measurement Data

COMMON CORE STANDARD—2.MD.9
Represent and interpret data.

1. Use an inch ruler.
   Measure and record the
   lengths of 4 different books
   in inches.

1st book: _____ inches
2nd book: _____ inches
3rd book: _____ inches
4th book: _____ inches

2. Make a line plot of the information above.
   Write a title for a line plot. Then
   write the numbers and draw the **X**s.

Problem Solving · Real World

3. Jesse measured the lengths of some strings.
   Use his list to complete the line plot.

Lengths of Strings
5 inches
7 inches
6 inches
8 inches
5 inches

Lesson Check (2.MD.9)

1. Use the line plot. How many sticks are 4 inches long?

Lengths of Sticks in Inches

_____ sticks

Spiral Review (2.NBT.7, 2.MD.1, 2.MD.3, 2.MD.5, 2.MD.6)

2. Kim wants to measure a ball. Circle the best tool for Kim to use.

counter   pencil

paper clip   measuring tape

3. Estimate how many 12 inch rulers will be about the same length as a teacher's desk.

_____ rulers, or _____ feet

4. Kurt has a string that is 12 inches long and another string that is 5 inches long. How many inches of string does he have altogether?

_____ inches

5. One box has 147 books. The other box has 216 books. How many books are there in both boxes?

_____ books

School-Home Letter

Dear Family,

My class started Chapter 9 this week. In this chapter, I will learn how to measure using centimeters and meters. I will also solve problems about adding and subtracting lengths.

Love, _____

Vocabulary

centimeter Unit of length

centimeters

meter 100 centimeters

Home Activity

Show your child an object that is about ten centimeters long. Have your child choose three or four more objects and estimate each length as more than ten centimeters or less than ten centimeters. Use the object that is about ten centimeters long to check your child's estimates.

Literature

Reading math stories reinforces ideas. Look for these books at the library.

How Tall, How Short, How Far Away? by David Adler. Holiday House, 2000.

Length by Henry Arthur Pluckrose. Children's Press, 1995.

Carta
para la **casa**

Querida familia:

Mi clase comenzó el Capítulo 9 esta semana. En este capítulo, aprenderé a medir usando centímetros y metros. También resolveré problemas de suma y resta de longitudes.

Con cariño, _____

Vocabulario

centímetro unidad de longitud

centímetros

metro 100 centímetros

Actividad para la casa

Muéstrele a su hijo un objeto de unos diez centímetros de largo. Pídale que elija tres o cuatro objetos más y que estime el largo de cada uno en más de diez centímetros o en menos de diez centímetros. Use el objeto de unos diezcentímetros de largo para comprobar las estimaciones de su hijo.

Literatura

Leer cuentos de matemáticas refuerza los conceptos. Busque estos libros en la biblioteca.

How Tall, How Short, How Far Away?
por David Adler.
Holiday House, 2000.

Length
por Henry Arthur Pluckrose.
Children's Press, 1995.

Measure with a Centimeter Model

COMMON CORE STANDARD—2.MD.1
Measure and estimate lengths in standard units.

Use a unit cube. Measure the length in centimeters.

1.

about _____ centimeters

2.

about _____ centimeters

3.

about _____ centimeters

4.

about _____ centimeters

Problem Solving *Real World*

Solve. Write or draw to explain.

5. Susan has a pencil that is 3 centimeters shorter than this string. How long is the pencil?

about _____ centimeters

1. Sarah used unit cubes to measure the length of a ribbon. Each unit cube is about 1 centimeter long. What is a good estimate for the length of ribbon?

_____ centimeters

Spiral Review (2.MD.5, 2.MD.6, 2.MD.7)

2. What is the time on this clock?

___ : ___

3. What is the time on this clock?

___ : ___

4. Dan has a paper strip that is 28 inches long. He tears 6 inches off the strip. How long is the paper strip now?

_____ inches

5. Rita has 1 quarter, 1 dime, and 2 pennies. What is the total value of Rita's coins?

$ _____ or _____ cents

Estimate Lengths in Centimeters

COMMON CORE STANDARD—2.MD.3
Measure and estimate lengths in standard units.

1. The toothpick is about 6 centimeters long. Circle the best estimate for the length of the yarn.

6 centimeters

9 centimeters

12 centimeters

2. The pen is about 11 centimeters long. Circle the best estimate for the length of the eraser.

4 centimeters

10 centimeters

14 centimeters

3. The string is about 6 centimeters long. Circle the best estimate for the length of the crayon.

5 centimeters

9 centimeters

14 centimeters

Problem Solving · Real World

4. The string is about 6 centimeters long. Draw a pencil that is about 12 centimeters long.

Lesson Check (2.MD.3)

1. The pencil is about 12 centimeters long. Estimate the length of the yarn.

_____ centimeters

Spiral Review (2.NBT.5, 2.MD.5, 2.MD.6, 2.MD.8)

2. Jeremy has 58 baseball cards. He gives 23 of them to his sister. How many baseball cards does Jeremy have left?

$$\begin{array}{r} 58 \\ -\ 23 \\ \hline \end{array}$$

_____ baseball cards

3. What is the sum?

$14 + 65 = $ _____

4. Adrian has a cube train that is 13 inches long. He adds 6 inches of cubes to the train. How long is the cube train now?

_____ inches

5. What is the total value of this group of coins?

$ _____, or _____ cents

Measure with a Centimeter Ruler

COMMON CORE STANDARD—2.MD.1
Measure and estimate lengths in standard units.

Measure the length to the nearest centimeter.

1.

_____ centimeters

2.

_____ centimeters

3.

_____ centimeters

Problem Solving · Real World

4. Draw a string that is about 8 centimeters long.
   Then use a centimeter ruler to check the length.

Lesson Check (2.MD.1)

1. Use a centimeter ruler. What is the length of this pencil to the nearest centimeter?

_____ centimeters

Spiral Review (2.MD.7, 2.MD.8, 2.MD.9)

2. What is the time on this clock?

_____ : _____

3. What is the total value of this group of coins?

$ _____ or _____ cents

4. Use the line plot. How many pencils are 5 inches long?

_____ pencils

Lengths of Pencils in Inches

Problem Solving • Add and Subtract Lengths

COMMON CORE STANDARDS—2.MD.6,
2.MD.5 *Relate addition and subtraction to length.*

Draw a diagram. Write a number sentence using

a ▓ for the missing number. Then solve.

1. A straw is 20 centimeters long. Mr. Jones
cuts off 8 centimeters of the straw. How long
is the straw now?

_____

The straw is _____ centimeters long now.

2. Ella has a piece of blue yarn that is 14 centimeters long.
She has a piece of red yarn that is 9 centimeters long.
How many centimeters of yarn does she have altogether?

_____

She has _____ centimeters of yarn altogether.

Lesson Check (2.MD.6, 2.MD.5)

1. Tina has a paper clip chain that is 25 centimeters long. She takes off 8 centimeters of the chain. How long is the chain now?

_____ centimeters

Spiral Review (2.NBT.7, 2.MD.7, 2.MD.8)

2. What is the sum?

$$327$$
$$+145$$

3. What is another way to write the time half past 7?

_____ : _____

---

4. Molly has these coins in her pocket. How much money does she have in her pocket?

$ _____ or _____ cents

Centimeters and Meters

Measure to the nearest centimeter.
Then measure to the nearest meter.

Find the real object.	Measure.
1. bookcase	_____ centimeters _____ meters
2. window	_____ centimeters _____ meters
3. map	_____ centimeters _____ meters

Problem Solving

4. Sally will measure the length of a wall in both centimeters and meters. Will there be fewer centimeters or fewer meters? Explain.

_____

_____

Lesson Check (2.MD.2)

1. Use a centimeter ruler. What is the length of the toothbrush to the nearest centimeter?

_____ centimeters

Spiral Review (2.NBT.7, 2.MD.2, 2.MD.8)

2. List a group of coins that equals 65 cents.

_____

_____

3. Janet has a poster that is about 3 feet long. Fill in the blanks with the word inches or feet to make the statement true.

3 _____ is longer than

12 _____ .

4. Last week, 483 children checked books out from the library. This week, only 162 children checked books out from the library. How many children checked out library books in the last two weeks?

$$
\begin{array}{r}
483 \\
+\ 162 \\
\hline
\end{array}
$$

5. List a group of coins with a value of $1.00?

_____

_____

Estimate Lengths in Meters

COMMON CORE STANDARD—2.MD.3
Measure and estimate lengths in standard units.

Find the real object.
Estimate its length in meters.

1. poster

about _____ meters

2. chalkboard

about _____ meters

3. bookshelf

about _____ meters

 Problem Solving Real World

4. Barbara and Luke each placed 2 meter sticks end-to-end along the length of a large table. About how long is the table?

about _____ meters

Lesson Check (2.MD.3)

1. What is the best estimate for the length of a real baseball bat?

_____ meter

2. What is the best estimate for the length of a real couch?

_____ meters

Spiral Review (2.MD.1, 2.MD.8)

3. Sara has two $1 bills, 3 quarters, and 1 dime. How much money does she have?

$ _____ . _____

4. Use an inch ruler. What is the length of this straw to the nearest inch?

_____ inches

5. Scott has this money in his pocket. What is the total value of this money?

$ _____ . _____

Name _____

Measure and Compare Lengths

COMMON CORE STANDARD—2.MD.4
Measure and estimate lengths in standard units.

Measure the length of each object. Write a number sentence to find the difference between the lengths.

1.

_____ centimeters

_____ centimeters

_____ − _____ = _____
centimeters   centimeters   centimeters

The craft stick is _____ centimeters longer than the chalk.

2.

_____ centimeters

_____ centimeters

_____ − _____ = _____
centimeters   centimeters   centimeters

The string is _____ centimeters longer than the toothpick.

Problem Solving

Solve. Write or draw to explain.

3. A string is 11 centimeters long, a ribbon is 24 centimeters long, and a large paper clip is 5 centimeters long. How much longer is the ribbon than the string?

_____ centimeters longer

Lesson Check (2.MD.4)

1. How much longer is the marker than the paper clip? Circle the correct answer.

11 centimeters longer

10 centimeters longer

8 centimeters longer

5 centimeters longer

Spiral Review (2.MD.3, 2.MD.7, 2.MD.8)

2. What is the total value of these coins?

$ _____ or _____ cents

3. What is a reasonable estimate for the length of a real chalkboard?

_____ feet

4. Cindy leaves at half past 2. At what time does Cindy leave?

_____ : _____

School-Home Letter

Dear Family,

My class started Chapter 10 this week. In this chapter, I will learn about collecting data, making graphs, and interpreting the data.

Love, _____

Vocabulary

picture graph A graph that uses pictures to show data

Apples Sold					
Eric	●	●			
Deb	●	●	●	●	
Alex	●				

Key: Each ● stands for 1 apple.

bar graph A graph that uses bars to show data

Home Activity

Take your child on a walk in your neighborhood. Help your child make a tally chart to record how many people you see driving, walking, and biking. Then talk with your child about the information that is in your tally chart.

How People Are Moving	
How Moving	**Tally**
driving	⩽⩽⩽ ||
walking	||||
biking	||

Literature

Reading math stories reinforces learning. Look for these books at the library.

Tables and Graphs of Healthy Things by Joan Freese. Gareth Stevens Publishing, 2008.

Lemonade for Sale by Stuart J. Murphy. Harper Collins, 1998.

10

Carta
para la casa

Querida familia:

Mi clase comenzó el Capítulo 10 esta semana. En este capítulo, aprenderé a recolectar datos, hacer grá cas e interpretar datos.

Con cariño, _____

Vocabulario

pictografía una gráfica que usa ilustraciones para mostrar datos

Manzanas vendidas				
Eric	●	●		
Deb	●	●	●	●
Alex	●			

Clave: Cada ● representa 2 manzanas.

gráfica de barras una gráfica que usa barras para mostrar datos

Actividad para la casa

Lleve a pasear a su hijo por el vecindario. Ayúdelo a crear una tabla de conteo para anotar cuántas personas ven manejando, caminando y montando en bicicleta. Luego, conversen sobre la información que hay en la tabla de conteo.

Cómo se mueve la gente	
Se mueven	**Conteo**
manejando	⊮⊬ ΙΙ
caminando	ΙΙΙΙ
en bicicleta	ΙΙ

Literatura

Leer cuentos de matemáticas refuerza los conceptos. Busque estos libros en la biblioteca.

Table and Graphs of Healthy Things por Joan Freese. Gareth Stevens Publishing, 2008.

Lemonade for Sale por Stuart J. Murphy. Harper Collins, 1998.

Collect Data

COMMON CORE STANDARD—2.MD.10
Represent and interpret data.

1. Take a survey. Ask 10 classmates how they got to school. Use tally marks to show their choices.

How We Got to School	
Way	**Tally**
walk	
bus	
car	
bike	

_____

2. How many classmates rode in a bus to school?

_____ classmates

3. How many classmates rode in a car to school?

_____ classmates

4. In which way did the fewest classmates get to school?

_____

5. In which way did the most classmates get to school?

_____

6. Did more classmates get to school by walking or by riding in a car?

_____

How many more?

_____ more classmates

Lesson Check (2.MD.10)

1. Use the tally chart. Which color did the fewest children choose?

_____

Favorite Color	
Color	Tally
blue	|||
green	� HHT ||||
red	HHT ||
yellow	HHT	

Spiral Review (2.MD.5, 2.MD.6, 2.MD.7, 2.MD.8)

2. List a group of coins that have a value of $1.00.

_____

3. Jared has two ropes. Each rope is 9 inches long. How many inches of rope does he have in all?

_____ inches

---

4. The clock shows the time Lee got to school. At what time did she get to school?

_____ : _____

5. Liza finished studying at half past 3. What time did Liza finish studying?

_____ : _____

Read Picture Graphs

COMMON CORE STANDARD—2.MD.10
Represent and interpret data.

Use the picture graph to answer the questions.

Number of Books Read						
Ryan	📕	📕	📕	📕		
Gwen	📕	📕				
Anna	📕	📕	📕	📕	📕	📕
Henry	📕	📕	📕			

Key: Each 📕 stands for 1 book.

1. How many books in all did Henry and Anna read? _____ books

2. How many more books did Ryan read than Gwen? _____ more books

3. How many fewer books did Gwen read than Anna? _____ fewer books

4. How many books did the four children read in all? _____ books

Problem Solving Real World

Use the picture graph above. Write or draw to explain.

5. Carlos read 4 books. How many children
   read fewer books than Carlos?

_____ children

Lesson Check (2.MD.10)

1. Use the picture graph. Who has the most fish?

Our Fish					
Jane					
Will	🐟	🐟	🐟		
Gina	🐟	🐟	🐟	🐟	
Evan	🐟	🐟			

_____

Key: Each 🐟 stands for 1 fish.

Spiral Review (2.MD.1, 2.MD.7, 2.MD.8)

2. What is the time on this clock?

_____ : _____

3. Each unit cube is about 1 centimeter long. Which is the best estimate for the length of the paper clip?

_____ centimeters

4. What is the total value of this group of coins?

$ _____ or _____ cents

Make Picture Graphs

COMMON CORE STANDARD—2.MD.10
Represent and interpret data.

1. Use the tally chart to complete the picture graph.
Draw a ☺ for each child.

Favorite Cookie	
Cookie	**Tally**
chocolate	|||
oatmeal	|
peanut butter	⊞⊞
shortbread	||||

Favorite Cookie					
chocolate					
oatmeal					
peanut butter					
shortbread					

Key: Each ☺ stands for 1 child.

2. How many children chose chocolate? ____ children

3. How many fewer children chose oatmeal than
peanut butter? ____ fewer children

4. Which cookie did the most children choose?

_____

5. How many children in all chose a favorite cookie? ____ children

6. How many children chose oatmeal or shortbread? ____ children

Lesson Check (2.MD.10)

1. Use the picture graph. How many more rainy days were there in April than in May?

Number of Rainy Days					
March	☂	☂	☂	☂	☂
April	☂	☂	☂	☂	
May	☂	☂			

Key: Each ☂ stands for 1 day.

_____ days

Spiral Review (2.MD.1, 2.MD.8)

2. Rita has one $1 bill, 2 quarters, and 3 dimes. What is the total value of Rita's money?

$ _____

3. Lucas put 4 quarters and 3 nickels into his coin bank. How much money did Lucas put into his coin bank?

$ _____

4. Use a centimeter ruler. What is the length of this string to the nearest centimeter?

|—————|

_____ centimeters

5. What is the total value of this group of coins?

$ _____ or _____ cents

Name _____

Read Bar Graphs

COMMON CORE STANDARD—2.MD.10
Represent and interpret data.

Use the bar graph.

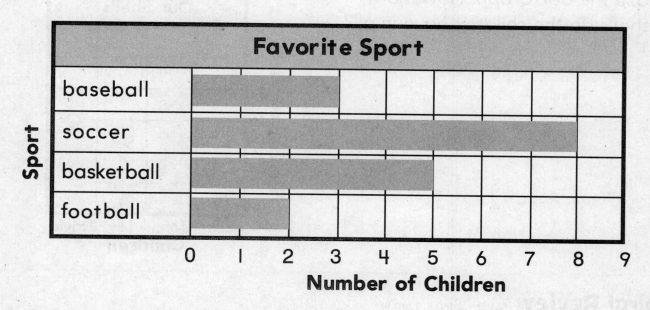

1. How many children chose basketball? _____ children

2. Which sport did the most children choose? _____

3. How many more children chose basketball
   than baseball? _____ more children

4. Which sport did the fewest children choose? _____

5. How many children chose a sport that was not soccer? _____ children

Problem Solving

6. How many children chose
   baseball or basketball?

   _____ children

Lesson Check (2.MD.10)

1. Use the bar graph. How many shells do the children have in all?

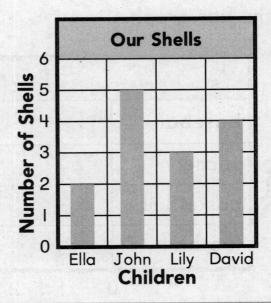

_____ shells

Spiral Review (2.MD.1, 2.MD.8, 2.MD.9)

2. Use the line plot. How many twigs are 3 inches long?

_____ twigs

```
                    X
   X        X               X
   X        X               X        X
   |_____|_____|_____|
   2        3       4        5
```

Lengths of Twigs in Inches

3. Use a centimeter ruler. What is the length of the yarn to the nearest centimeter?

_____ centimeters

4. Noah buys a pencil. He uses 1 quarter and 2 nickels to pay. How much money does the pencil cost?

$ _____ or _____ cents

Make Bar Graphs

COMMON CORE STANDARD—2.MD.10
Represent and interpret data.

Maria asked her friends how many hours they practice soccer each week.

- Jessie practices for 3 hours.
- Victor practices for 2 hours.
- Samantha practices for 5 hours.
- David practices for 6 hours.

1. Write a title and labels for the bar graph.

_____

2. Draw bars in the graph to show the data.

Jessie										
Victor										
Samantha										
David										

0 1 2 3 4 5 6 7 8 9 10

_____

3. Which friend practices soccer for the most hours each week?

_____

Problem Solving Real World

4. Which friends practice soccer for fewer than 4 hours each week?

_____

Lesson Check (2.MD.10)

1. Use the bar graph. How many more children chose summer than spring?

Favorite Season

Season							
summer							
fall							
winter							
spring							

0　1　2　3　4　5　6

Number of Children

_____ children

Spiral Review (2.MD.1, 2.MD.5, 2.MD.6, 2.MD.7, 2.MD.8)

2. Rachel's chain is 22 centimeters long. She takes 9 centimeters off the chain. How long is Rachel's chain now?

_____ centimeters

3. Use an inch ruler. What is the length of the yarn to the nearest inch?

_____ inches

4. Gail finished studying at quarter past 1. What time did Gail finish studying?

_____ : _____

5. Jill has two $1 bills, 1 quarter, and 1 nickel. How much money does Jill have?

$ _____

Problem Solving • Display Data

COMMON CORE STANDARD—2.MD.10
Represent and interpret data.

Make a bar graph to solve the problem.

I. The list shows the number of books that Abby read each month. Describe how the number of books she read changed from February to May.

February	8 books
March	7 books
April	6 books
May	4 books

	0	1	2	3	4	5	6	7	8	9	10
February											
March											
April											
May											

The number of books _____

_____

_____

2. How many books in all did Abby read in February and March?

_____ books

3. How many fewer books did Abby read in April than in February?

_____ fewer books

4. In which months did Abby read fewer than 7 books?

_____

Lesson Check (2.MD.10)

1. Use the bar graph. Describe how the number of hours changed from Week 1 to Week 4.

The number of hours _____.

Hours at Practice

Spiral Review (2.MD.3, 2.MD.8)

2. The string is about 10 centimeters long. Estimate the length of the feather.

_____ centimeters

3. What is the total value of this group of coins?

$ _____ or _____ cents

4. Rick has one $1 bill, 2 dimes, and 3 pennies. How much money does Rick have?

$ _____

School-Home Letter

Dear Family:

My class started Chapter 11 this week. In this chapter, I will learn about three-dimensional and two-dimensional shapes. I will also learn about equal parts of a whole.

Love, _____

Vocabulary

quadrilateral

cone

pentagon

cylinder

hexagon

cube

Home Activity

Name a two-dimensional shape: triangle, quadrilateral, pentagon, or hexagon. With your child, look for an object that has that shape.

Repeat the activity using a three-dimensional shape: cube, rectangular prism, sphere, cylinder, or cone.

Literature

Reading math stories reinforces learning. Look for these books at the library.

Shape Up! by David Adler. Holiday House, 1998.

The Village of Round and Square Houses by Ann Grifalconi. Little, Brown and Company, 1986.

Carta para la casa

Querida familia:

Mi clase comenzó hoy el Capítulo 11. En este capítulo, aprenderé acerca de las guras bidimensionales y tridimensionales. También aprenderé sobre las partes igualdades de un entero.

Con cariño, _____

Vocabulario

cuadrilátero

pentágono

hexágono

cono

cilindro

cubo

Actividad para la casa

Nombre alguna figura bidimensional, como triángulo, cuadrilátero, pentágono o hexágono. Juntos, busquen una figura que tenga la misma forma. Repitan la actividad con una figura tridimensional, como cubo, prisma rectangular, esfera, cilindro o cono.

Literatura

Leer cuentos de matemáticas refuerza el aprendizaje. Busquen estos libros en la biblioteca.

Shape Up! por David Adler. Holiday House, 1998

The Village of Round and Square Houses por Ann Grifalconi. Little, Brown and Company, 1986.

Three-Dimensional Shapes

COMMON CORE STANDARD—2.G.1
Reason with shapes and their attributes.

Circle the objects that match the shape name.

1. cube			
2. cone			
3. rectangular prism			
4. cylinder			

Problem Solving Real World

5. Lisa draws a circle by tracing around the bottom of a block. Which could be the shape of Lisa's block? Circle the name of the shape.

cone   cube   rectangular prism

© Houghton Mifflin Harcourt Publishing Company

Lesson Check (2.G.1)

1. What is the name of this shape?

_____

2. What is the name of this shape?

_____

Spiral Review (2.MD.3, 2.MD.7, 2.MD.8)

3. The string is about 6 centimeters long. What is a reasonable estimate for the length of the crayon?

_____ centimeters

4. What is the total value of this group of coins?

_____

5. What time is shown on this clock?

_____ : _____

Name _____

Build Three-Dimensional Shapes

Build a rectangular prism with the given number of unit cubes. Shade to show the top and front views.

COMMON CORE STANDARD—2.G.1
Recognize and draw shapes having specified attributes, such as a given number of angles or a given number of equal faces. Identify triangles, quadrilaterals, pentagons, hexagons, and cubes.

	top view	front view
I. 12 unit cubes		

Problem Solving Real World

Solve. Write or draw to explain.

2. Rosie built this rectangular prism. How many unit cubes did she use?

_____ unit cubes

Lesson Check (2.G.1)

3. Milt builds the first layer of a rectangular prism using 3 cubes. He adds 2 more layers of 3 cubes each. How many cubes are used for the prism?

_____ cubes

4. Thea builds the first layer of a rectangular prism using 4 cubes. Raj adds 4 more layers of 4 cubes each. How many cubes are used for the prism?

_____ cubes

Spiral Review (2.MD.7, 2.NBT.7.1, 2.MD.10, 2.MD.10)

5. Patti's dance class will meet for 1 year. Her art class will meet for 32 weeks. Which is the greater amount of time?

_____

6. A large pack has 512 beads. A small pack has 346 beads. Estimate how many more beads the large pack has than the small pack.

about _____ more beads

Use the bar graph.

7. Which kind of fruit got the fewest votes?

_____

8. How many more votes did grape get than apple?

_____ more votes

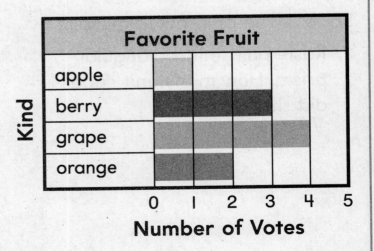

Name _____

Two-Dimensional Shapes

 COMMON CORE STANDARD—2.G.1
Reason with shapes and their attributes.

Write the number of sides and the number of vertices. Then write the name of the shape.

pentagon   triangle

hexagon   quadrilateral

1.

_____ sides

_____ vertices

_____

2.

_____ sides

_____ vertices

_____

3.

_____ sides

_____ vertices

_____

4.

_____ sides

_____ vertices

_____

5.

_____ sides

_____ vertices

_____

6.

_____ sides

_____ vertices

_____

Problem Solving

Solve. Draw or write to explain.

7. Oscar is drawing a picture of a house.
He draws a pentagon shape for a window.
How many sides does his window have?

_____ sides

Lesson Check (2.G.1)

1. How many sides does a hexagon have?

_____ sides

2. How many vertices does a quadrilateral have?

_____ vertices

Spiral Review (2.MD.1, 2.MD.10)

3. Use a centimeter ruler. What is the length of the ribbon to the nearest centimeter?

_____ centimeters

4. Look at the picture graph. How many more children chose apples than oranges?

_____ children

Favorite Fruit					
apples	☺	☺	☺	☺	
oranges	☺	☺			
grapes	☺	☺	☺		
peaches	☺	☺			

Key: Each ☺ stands for 1 child.

Angles in Two-Dimensional Shapes

COMMON CORE STANDARD—2.G.1
Reason with shapes and their attributes.

**Circle the angles in each shape.
Write how many.**

1.

_____ angles

2.

_____ angles

3.

_____ angles

4.

_____ angles

Problem Solving Real World

5. Logan drew 2 two-dimensional shapes that had
8 angles in all. Draw shapes Logan could have drawn.

Lesson Check (2.G.1)

1. How many angles does this shape have?

_____ angles

2. How many angles does this shape have?

_____ angles

Spiral Review (2.MD.5, 2.MD.6, 2.MD.10, 2.G.1)

3. Use an inch ruler. What is the length of the string to the nearest inch?

_____ inches

4. Look at the picture graph. How many children chose daisies?

_____ children

Favorite Flower					
roses	☺	☺	☺	☺	
tulips	☺	☺	☺		
daisies	☺	☺	☺	☺	☺
lillies	☺	☺			

Key: Each ☺ stands for 1 child.

Sort Two-Dimensional Shapes

COMMON CORE STANDARD—2.G.1
Reason with shapes and their attributes.

Circle the shapes that match the rule.

1. Shapes with fewer than 5 sides

2. Shapes with more than 4 sides

3. Shapes with 4 angles

4. Shapes with fewer than 6 angles

Problem Solving · Real World

Circle the correct shape.

5. Tammy drew a shape with more than 3 angles.
It is not a hexagon. Which shape did Tammy draw?

Lesson Check (2.G.1)

1. Which shape has fewer than 4 sides?

Spiral Review (2.MD.1, 2.MD.10)

2. Use an inch ruler. What is the length of the pencil to the nearest inch?

_____ inches

---

3. Use the tally chart. How many children chose basketball as their favorite sport?

_____ children

Favorite Sport	
Sport	Tally
soccer	卌
basketball	卌 II
football	IIII
baseball	IIII

Partition Rectangles

Use color tiles to cover the rectangle.
Trace around the square tiles.
Write how many.

COMMON CORE STANDARD—2.G.2
Reason with shapes and their attributes.

1.

Number of rows: _____

Number of columns: _____

Total: _____ square tiles

2.

Number of rows: _____

Number of columns: _____

Total: _____ square tiles

Problem Solving Real World

Solve. Write or draw to explain.

3. Nina wants to put color tiles on a square. 3 color tiles fit across the top of the square. How many rows and columns of of squares will Nina need? How many color tiles will she use in all?

Number of rows: _____

Number of columns: _____

Total: _____ square tiles

_____ tiles

Lesson Check (2.G.2)

1. Use color tiles to cover the rectangle. How many tiles did you use?

_____ tiles

Spiral Review (2.MD.10, 2.G.1)

2. How many faces does a cube have?

_____ faces

3. How many angles does this shape have?

_____ angles

4. Use the tally chart. How many more children chose art than reading?

_____ children

Favorite Subject	
Subject	Tally
reading	卌 |||
math	卌 ||||
science	卌
art	卌 卌

Equal Parts

COMMON CORE STANDARD—2.G.3
Reason with shapes and their attributes.

Write how many equal parts there are in the whole.
Write halves, thirds, or fourths to name the equal parts.

1.

_____ equal parts

_____

2.

_____ equal parts

_____

3.

_____ equal parts

_____

4.

_____ equal parts

_____

5.

_____ equal parts

_____

6.

_____ equal parts

_____

Problem Solving Real World

7. Sort the shapes.

   • Draw an X on the shapes
     that do not show equal parts.

   • Circle the shapes that
     show halves.

Lesson Check (2.G.3)

1. What are the 3 equal parts of the shape called?

_____

2. What are the 4 equal parts of the shape called?

_____

Spiral Review (2.NBT.5, 2.G.1)

3. What is the sum?

$$87 + 45$$

4. What is the difference?

$$59 - 15$$

5. Circle the quadrilateral.

6. Circle the hexagon.

Show Equal Parts of a Whole

COMMON CORE STANDARD—2.G.3
Reason with shapes and their attributes.

Draw to show equal parts.

1. halves

2. fourths

3. thirds

4. thirds

5. halves

6. fourths

7. fourths

8. halves

9. thirds

Problem Solving Real World

Solve. Write or draw to explain.

10. Joe has one sandwich. He cuts the sandwich into fourths. How many pieces of sandwich does he have?

_____ pieces

Lesson Check (2.G.3)

1. Circle the shape divided into fourths.

Spiral Review (2.MD.4, 2.G.1)

2. How many angles does this shape have?

_____ angles

3. How many faces does a rectangular prism have?

_____ faces

4. Use a centimeter ruler. Measure the length of each object. How much longer is the ribbon than the string?

_____ centimeters long

Describe Equal Parts

COMMON CORE STANDARD—2.G.3
Reason with shapes and their attributes.

Draw to show halves.
Color a half of the shape.

1.

2.

Draw to show thirds.
Color a third of the shape.

3.

4.

Draw to show fourths.
Color a fourth of the shape.

5.

6.

Problem Solving Real World

7. Circle all the shapes that have a third of the shape shaded.

    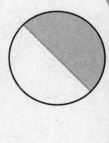

Lesson Check (2.G.3)

1. Circle the shape that is half shaded.

   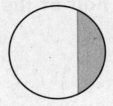

Spiral Review (2.MD.1, 2.MD.7, 2.G.1)

2. What is the name of this shape?

_____

3. Use a centimeter ruler. What is the length of the string to the nearest centimeter?

_____ centimeters

4. The clock shows the time Chris finished his homework. What time did Chris finish his homework?

____ : ____ ____

5. What time is shown on this clock?

____ : ____

Problem Solving • Equal Shares

COMMON CORE STANDARD—2.G.3
Reason with shapes and their attributes.

Draw to show your answer.

1. Max has square pizzas that are the same size.
   What are two different ways he can divide the
   pizzas into fourths?

2. Lia has two pieces of paper that are the same size.
   What are two different ways she can divide the
   pieces of paper into halves?

3. Frank has two crackers that are the same size.
   What are two different ways he can divide the
   cracker into thirds?

Lesson Check (2.G.3)

1. Bree cut a piece of cardboard into thirds like this.

Circle the other shape that is divided into thirds.

Spiral Review (2.MD.7, 2.MD.8, 2.G.1)

2. Circle the shape with three equal parts.

3. How many angles does this shape have?

_____ angles

---

4. What is the best estimate for the width of a door?

_____ feet

5. Which is another way to write 10 minutes after 9?

_____ : _____

Find Sums on an Addition Table

Essential Question How do you find sums on an addition table?

Model and Draw

$3 + 4 = ?$

The sum for $3 + 4$ is found where row 3 and column 4 meet.

$3 + 4 = \underline{7}$

+	0	1	2	3	④ column
0	0	1	2	3	4
1	1	2	3	4	5
2	2	3	4	5	6
③ row	3	4	5	6	⑦
4	4	5	6	7	8

Share and Show

 MATH BOARD

1. Write the missing sums in the addition table.

+	0	1	2	3	4	5	6	7	8	9	10
0	0	1	2	3	4	5	6			9	
1	1	2	3	4	5	6			9		11
2	2	3	4	5	6			9		11	12
3	3	4	5	6			9		11	12	13
4	4	5	6			9		11	12	13	14
5	5	6			9		11	12	13	14	15
6	6			9		11	12	13	14	15	16
7			9		11	12	13	14	15	16	17
8		9		11	12	13	14	15	16	17	18
9	9		11	12	13	14	15	16	17	18	19
10		11	12	13	14	15	16	17	18	19	20

 Math Talk Describe a pattern in the addition table.

2. Write the missing sums in the addition table.

+	0	1	2	3	4	5	6	7	8	9	10
0	0	1	2	3	4	5	6	7	8	9	10
1	1	2	3	4	5	6	7	8	9	10	
2	2	3	4	5	6	7	8	9	10		12
3	3	4	5	6	7	8	9	10		12	
4	4	5	6	7	8	9	10		12		
5	5	6	7	8	9	10		12			15
6	6	7	8	9	10		12			15	16
7	7	8	9	10		12			15	16	17
8	8	9	10		12			15	16	17	18
9	9	10		12			15	16	17	18	19
10	10		12			15	16	17	18	19	20

Problem Solving Real World

Solve. Write or draw to explain.

3. Natasha has 13 apples. Some apples are red and some are green. She has more red apples than green apples. How many red apples and how many green apples could she have?

TAKE HOME ACTIVITY • Ask your child to explain how to use the addition table to find the sum of 8 + 6.

Make and Use a Ruler

COMMON CORE STANDARD—2.MD.1
Measure and estimate lengths in standard units.

Measure the length with your ruler.
Count the inches.

1.

about _____ inches

2.

about _____ inches

3.

about _____ inches

4.

about _____ inches

Problem Solving Real World

5. Use your ruler. Measure the width
of this page in inches.

about _____ inches

Lesson Check (2.MD.1)

1. Use your ruler. What is the length of this ribbon?

about _____ inches

Spiral Review (2.OA.4, 2.NBT.7, 2.MD.7, 2.MD.8)

2. What time is shown on this clock?

_____ : _____

3. What is the total value of these coins?

_____ cents

4. The first group collected 238 cans. The second group collected 345 cans. How many cans did the two groups collect?

_____

5. There are 2 children in each row. How many children are in 5 rows?

_____ children

Estimate Sums: 2-Digit Addition

Essential Question How can you estimate the sum
of two 2-digit numbers?

Model and Draw

Estimate the sum of 24 + 38.
Find the nearest ten for each number.

___20___ + ___40___ = ___60___

An estimate of the sum is ___60___.

Share and Show

Find the nearest ten for each number.

1. Estimate the sum of 18 + 29.

Add the tens to estimate.

_____ + _____ = _____

An estimate of the sum is _____.

Math Talk   How did you know which
ten is nearest to 18?

On Your Own

Find the nearest ten for each number.
Add the tens to estimate.

2. Estimate the sum of 13 + 28.

10 11 12 13 14 15 16 17 18 19 **20** 21 22 23 24 25 26 27 28 29 **30**

_____ + _____ = _____

An estimate of the sum is _____.

---

3. Estimate the sum of 31 + 22.

20 21 22 23 24 25 26 27 28 29 **30** 31 32 33 34 35 36 37 38 39 **40**

_____ + _____ = _____

An estimate of the sum is _____.

Problem Solving

Solve. Write or draw to explain.

4. Mark has 34 pennies. Emma has 47 pennies.
About how many pennies do they have
altogether?

about _____ pennies

TAKE HOME ACTIVITY • Ask your child to use the number line for Exercise 2
and describe how to estimate the sum of 27 + 21.

Estimate Sums: 3-Digit Addition

Essential Question How can you estimate the sum of two 3-digit numbers?

Model and Draw

Estimate the sum of 189 + 284.
Find the nearest hundred for each number.

100   150   **200**   250   **300**
         ↑189   ↑284

_200_ + _300_ = _500_

An estimate of the sum is __500__.

Share and Show

Find the nearest hundred for each number.
Add the hundreds to estimate.

I. Estimate the sum of 229 + 386.

200   250   **300**   350   **400**

_____ + _____ = _____

An estimate of the sum is _____.

Math Talk   How do you know which two hundreds a 3-digit number is between?

On Your Own

Find the nearest hundred for each number.
Add the hundreds to estimate.

2. Estimate the sum of 324 + 218.

200   250   300   350   400

_____ + _____ = _____

An estimate of the sum is _____.

3. Estimate the sum of 468 + 439.

300   350   400   450   500

_____ + _____ = _____

An estimate of the sum is _____.

Problem Solving

Solve. Write or draw to explain.

4. There are 375 yellow fish and 283 blue fish
swimming around a coral reef. About
how many fish are there altogether?

about _____ fish

TAKE HOME ACTIVITY • Ask your child to use the number line for
Exercise 2 and describe how to estimate the sum of 215 + 398.

Estimate Differences: 2-Digit Subtraction

Essential Question How can you estimate the difference of two 2-digit numbers?

Estimate the difference of 62 − 48.
Find the nearest ten for each number.

$$\underline{\quad 60 \quad} - \underline{\quad 50 \quad} = \underline{\quad 10 \quad}$$

An estimate of the difference is ____10____.

Share and Show

MATH BOARD

Find the nearest ten for each number.
Subtract the tens to estimate.

1. Estimate the difference of 42 − 29.

$$\underline{\quad\quad\quad} - \underline{\quad\quad\quad} = \underline{\quad\quad\quad}$$

An estimate of the difference is _____.

Math Talk   How do you know which two tens a number is between?

Find the nearest ten for each number.
Subtract the tens to estimate.

2. Estimate the difference of 51 − 39.

30 31 32 33 34 35 36 37 38 39 **40** 41 42 43 44 45 46 47 48 49 **50** 51 52 53 54 55 56 57 58 59 **60**

_____ − _____ = _____

An estimate of the difference is _____.

3. Estimate the difference of 79 − 56.

50 51 52 53 54 55 56 57 58 59 **60** 61 62 63 64 65 66 67 68 69 **70** 71 72 73 74 75 76 77 78 79 **80**

_____ − _____ = _____

An estimate of the difference is _____.

Problem Solving

Solve. Write or draw to explain.

4. A farmer has 91 cows. 58 of the cows
are in the barn. About how many of the
cows are not in the barn?

about _____ cows

TAKE HOME ACTIVITY • Ask your child to use the number line for Exercise 2
and describe how to estimate the difference of 57 − 41.

Estimate Differences: 3-Digit Subtraction

Essential Question How can you estimate the difference of two 3-digit numbers?

Model and Draw

Estimate the difference of 382 − 265.
Find the nearest hundred for each number.

__400__ − __300__ = __100__

An estimate of the difference is __100__.

Share and Show

Find the nearest hundred for each number.
Subtract the hundreds to estimate.

I. Estimate the difference of 674 − 590.

_____ − _____ = _____

An estimate of the difference is _____.

 Math Talk How did you know which hundred is nearest to 674?

Find the nearest hundred for each number.
Subtract the hundreds to estimate.

2. Estimate the difference of 791 − 612.

600   650   **700**   750   **800**

_____ − _____ = _____

An estimate of the difference is _____.

---

3. Estimate the difference of 487 − 309.

300   350   **400**   450   **500**

_____ − _____ = _____

An estimate of the difference is _____.

Problem Solving

Solve. Write or draw to explain.

4. A mail carrier had 819 letters to deliver.
Then she delivered 687 letters. About how
many letters does she still have to deliver?

about _____ letters

TAKE HOME ACTIVITY • Ask your child to use the number line for Exercise 2
and describe how to estimate the difference of 786 − 611.

Name _____

Order 3-Digit Numbers

Essential Question: How does place value help you order 3-digit numbers?

Model and Draw

You can order 249, 418, and 205 from least to greatest. First, compare the **hundreds**. Next, compare the tens and then the ones, if needed.

Hundreds	Tens	Ones
2	4	9
4	1	8
2	0	5

I compare the hundreds. 249 and 205 are both less than 418.

Which is less, 249 or 205? I compare the tens. 205 is less than 249, so 205 is the least.

$$\underset{\text{least}}{\underline{205}} < \underline{249} < \underset{\text{greatest}}{\underline{418}}$$

Share and Show

Write the numbers in order from least to greatest.

1.

```
6 7 2
5 1 5
5 3 2
```

_____ < _____ < _____

2.

```
7 8 7
6 8 3
5 6 4
```

_____ < _____ < _____

Math Talk   Do you always need to compare the ones digits when you order numbers? Explain.

Write the numbers in order from least to greatest.

3.

```
3 5 9
7 1 5
6 0 8
```

___ < ___ < ___

4.

```
9 5 9
9 1 5
9 0 8
```

___ < ___ < ___

5.

```
3 4 3
3 4 1
3 4 8
```

___ < ___ < ___

6.

```
1 6 5
7 4 6
7 6 4
```

___ < ___ < ___

Problem Solving Real World

7. Brenda, Jean, and Pam play a video game. Brenda scores the highest. Jean scores the lowest.

Brenda	8 6 3
Jean	7 6 7
Pam	?

On the line, write a 3-digit number that could be Pam's score.

767 < _____ < 863

TAKE HOME ACTIVITY • Write three 3-digit numbers. Have your child tell you how to order the numbers from least to greatest.

Name _____

✓ Checkpoint

Concepts and Skills

1. Write the missing sums in the addition table.

+	0	1	2	3	4	5	6	7	8	9	10
0	0	1	2	3	4	5		7		9	
1	1	2	3	4	5		7		9		11
2	2	3	4	5		7		9		11	12
3	3	4	5		7		9		11	12	13
4	4	5		7		9		11	12	13	14
5	5		7		9		11	12	13	14	15

Find the nearest ten.

2. Estimate the sum of 24 and 36.

20 21 22 23 24 25 26 27 28 29 **30** 31 32 33 34 35 36 37 38 39 **40**

_____ + _____ = _____

An estimate of the sum is _____.

Find the nearest hundred.

3. Estimate the sum of 285 and 122.

100   150   **200**   250   **300**

_____ + _____ = _____

An estimate of the sum is _____.

Find the nearest ten.

4. Estimate the difference of 72 − 59.

___ − ___ = ___

An estimate of the difference is ___.

Find the nearest hundred.

5. Estimate the difference of 792 and 619.

___ − ___ = ___

An estimate of the difference is ___.

6. Which of the following numbers will make this true?

350 < 413 < _____.

○ 403

○ 398

○ 430

○ 331

Equal Groups of 2

Essential Question: How can you find the total number in equal groups of 2?

Model and Draw

The pet store has 3 fishbowls in the window. There are 2 goldfish in each bowl. How many goldfish are there in all?

Make 3 groups of 2 counters.

__3__ groups of __2__ is __6__ in all.

> I can count the equal groups by twos—2, 4, 6—to find how many in all.

Share and Show

MATH BOARD

Complete the sentence to show how many in all.

1.

_____ groups of _____ is _____ in all.

2.

_____ groups of _____ is _____ in all.

3.

_____ groups of _____ is _____ in all.

 Math Talk   How can you use counters to find 2 + 2 + 2 + 2 + 2?

Complete the sentence to show how many in all.

4.

_____ groups of _____ is _____ in all.

5.

_____ groups of _____ is _____ in all.

6.

_____ groups of _____ is _____ in all.

7.

_____ groups of _____ is _____ in all.

Problem Solving Real World

Solve. Write or draw to explain.

8. Coach Baker keeps 2 basketballs in each bin. There are 5 bins. How many basketballs are stored in the bins?

_____ basketballs

© Houghton Mifflin Harcourt Publishing Company

 TAKE HOME ACTIVITY • Have your child draw groups of two Xs and tell you how to find how many there are in all.

Equal Groups of 5

Essential Question: How can you find the total number in equal groups of 5?

Model and Draw

Luke made 3 cube trains. He connected 5 cubes in each train. How many cubes did he use in all?

Make 3 groups of 5 cubes.

I can count the equal groups by fives—5, 10, 15—to find how many in all.

__3__ groups of __5__ is __15__ in all.

Share and Show

MATH BOARD

Complete the sentence to show how many in all.

1.

____ groups of ____ is ____ in all.

2.

____ groups of ____ is ____ in all.

3.

____ groups of ____ is ____ in all.

 Math Talk   How can you use addition to find how many in all in Exercise 2?

Complete the sentences to show how many in all.

4.

____ groups of ____ is ____ in all.

5.

____ groups of ____ is ____ in all.

6.

____ groups of ____ is ____ in all.

Problem Solving

Solve. Write or draw to explain.

7. Gina fills 6 pages of her photo album. She puts 5 photos on each page. How many photos does Gina put in her album?

____ photos

 TAKE HOME ACTIVITY • Place your hands next to your child's hands. Ask how many groups of 5 fingers. Have your child tell you how to find how many in all. How many fingers in all?

Equal Groups of 10

Essential Question: How can you find the total number in equal groups of 10?

Model and Draw

There are 4 packs of juice. Each pack has 10 juice boxes. How many juice boxes are there in all?

Make 4 groups of 10 cubes.

> I can count the equal groups by tens—10, 20, 30, 40—to find how many in all.

__4__ groups of __10__ is __40__ in all.

Share and Show

MATH BOARD

Complete the sentence to show how many in all.

1.

____ groups of ____ is ____ in all.

2.

____ groups of ____ is ____ in all.

3.

____ groups of ____ is ____ in all.

 Math Talk How many groups of ten are in 70?
Explain.

Complete the sentence to show how many in all.

4.

_____ groups of _____ is _____ in all.

5.

_____ groups of _____ is _____ in all.

6.

_____ groups of _____ is _____ in all.

Problem Solving

Solve. Write or draw to explain.

7. To count his pennies, Travis puts 10 pennies in a stack. He makes 4 stacks. How many pennies does Travis have?

_____ pennies

© Houghton Mifflin Harcourt Publishing Company

 TAKE HOME ACTIVITY • Give your child 30 pieces of macaroni or other small objects. Have your child make groups of 10. Ask how many groups there are. Ask your child to tell you how to find how many in all. How many pieces in all?

Name _____

Size of Shares

Essential Question How can you place items in equal groups?

Model and Draw

When you divide, you place items in equal groups.

Joel has 12 carrots. There are 6 rabbits. Each rabbit gets the same number of carrots. How many carrots does each rabbit get?

Place 12 counters in 6 equal groups.

_2_ counters in each group   So, each rabbit gets _2_ carrots.

Share and Show

Use counters. Draw to show your work.
Write how many in each group.

1. Place 10 counters in 2 equal groups.

_____ counters in each group

_____

2. Place 6 counters in 3 equal groups.

_____ counters in each group

Math Talk   How did you know how many counters to place in each group for Exercise 2?

Use counters. Draw to show your work.
Write how many in each group.

3. Place 9 counters in 3 equal groups.

_____ counters in each group

4. Place 12 counters in 2 equal groups.

_____ counters in each group

5. Place 16 counters in 4 equal groups.

_____ counters in each group

Problem Solving

Solve. Draw to show your work.

6. Mrs. Peters divides 6 orange slices
between 2 plates. She wants to have
4 orange slices on each plate. How many
more orange slices does she need?

_____ more orange slices

TAKE HOME ACTIVITY • Ask your child to place 15 pennies into
3 equal groups, and then tell how many pennies are in each group.

Name _____

Number of Equal Shares

Essential Question How can you find the number of equal groups that items can be placed into?

Model and Draw

There are 12 cookies. 3 cookies fill a snack bag. How many snack bags can be filled?

Place 12 counters in groups of 3.

___4___ groups

So, ___4___ snack bags can be filled.

Share and Show

Use counters. Draw to show your work.
Write how many groups.

1. Place 8 counters in groups of 4.

_____ groups

2. Place 10 counters in groups of 2.

_____ groups

Math Talk **Describe** how you could find the number of groups of 2 you could make with 12 counters.

Use counters. Draw to show your work.
Write how many groups.

3. Place 4 counters in groups of 2.

_____ groups

4. Place 12 counters in groups of 4.

_____ groups

5. Place 15 counters in groups of 3.

_____ groups

Problem Solving Real World

Draw to show your work.

6. Some children want to play a board
game. There are 16 game pieces.
Each player needs to have 4 pieces.
How many children can play?

_____ children

TAKE HOME ACTIVITY • Use small items such as pennies or cereal. Have your
child find out how many groups of 5 are in 20.

Solve Problems with Equal Shares

Essential Question: How can you solve word problems that involve equal shares?

Model and Draw

You can draw a picture to help you solve problems with equal shares.

There are 10 marbles in each bag. How many marbles are in 3 bags?

____10____   ____10____   ____10____

__3__ groups of __10__ is __30__ in all.

There are __30__ marbles.

Share and Show

Solve. Draw or write to show what you did.

1. There are 5 oranges in each sack. How many oranges are in 4 sacks?

_____ oranges

2. Sandy can plant 2 seeds in a pot. How many pots will Sandy need in order to plant 6 seeds?

_____ pots

Math Talk   Explain how you solved Exercise 2.

Solve. Draw to show what you did.

3. Ben gives each friend 2 crackers. How many crackers does he need for 6 friends?

_____ crackers

4. Mrs. Green can pack 5 books in a box. How many boxes will she need in order to pack 15 books?

_____ boxes

Problem Solving

5. Franco used 12 connecting cubes to build towers. All the towers are the same height. Draw a picture to show the towers he could have built.

TAKE HOME ACTIVITY • Ask your child to make up a word problem about 3 boxes of toys with 3 toys in each box. Have your child tell you how to solve the problem.

Name _____

✓ Checkpoint

Complete the sentence to show how many in all.

1.

____ groups of ____ is ____ in all.

2.

____ groups of ____ is ____ in all.

3.

____ groups of ____ is ____ in all.

Use counters. Draw to show your work.
Write how many in each group.

4. Place 14 counters in 2 equal groups.

_____ counters in each group

Use counters. Draw to show your work.
Write how many groups.

5. Place 12 counters in groups of 2.

_____ groups

Solve the problem.

6. Mrs. Owen puts 3 flowers in each vase.
How many flowers are in 4 vases?

○ 7

○ 9

○ 12

○ 16

Hour Before and Hour After

Essential Question: How do you tell the time 1 hour before and 1 hour after a given time?

Model and Draw

For these times, the minute hand points to the same place. The hour hands point to different numbers.

The time is <u>8:00</u>.

The hour hand points to 8.

1 hour before

<u>7:00</u>

The hour hand points to 7.

1 hour after

<u>9:00</u>

The hour hand points to 9.

Share and Show

MATH BOARD

Write the time shown on the clock. Then write the time 1 hour before and 1 hour after.

1.

_____ 1 hour before

_____ 1 hour after

2.

_____ 1 hour before

_____ 1 hour after

Math Talk How are the hands on a clock that shows 8 o'clock the same as the hands on a clock 1 hour after? How are they different?

Write the time shown. Then write the time I hour
before and I hour after.

3.

_____
I hour before

_____
I hour after

4.

_____
I hour before

_____
I hour after

5.

_____
I hour before

_____
I hour after

6.

_____
I hour before

_____
I hour after

Problem Solving

7. Tim feeds the cat I hour after 7:00.
Draw the hour hand and the minute
hand to show I hour after 7:00. Then
write the time.

Tim needs to feed the cat at _____.

 TAKE HOME ACTIVITY • Ask your child what the time will be I hour after
3:30. What time was it I hour before 3:30? Have your child tell you how he or
she knows.

Elapsed Time in Hours

Essential Question How do you find the number of hours between two times?

Model and Draw

Baseball practice starts at 2:00. Everyone leaves practice at 4:00. How long does baseball practice last?
Use the time line to count how many hours passed from 2:00 P.M. to 4:00 P.M.

Starts at 2:00   **Ends at 4:00**

_____ hours

9:00 A.M.   11:00 A.M.   1:00 P.M.   3:00 P.M.   5:00 P.M.

10:00 A.M.   Noon   2:00 P.M.   4:00 P.M.   6:00 P.M.

Share and Show

Use the time line above. Solve.

1. The game starts at 3:00 P.M. It ends at 6:00 P.M. How long does the game last?

   _____ hours

2. The plane leaves at 10:00 A.M. It arrives at 2:00 P.M. How long is the plane trip?

   _____ hours

3. Max goes out at 2:00 P.M. He comes back in at 5:00 P.M. For how long was Max out?

   _____ hours

4. Art class starts at 9:00 A.M. It ends at 11:00 A.M. How long is the art class?

   _____ hours

Math Talk   Describe how you used the time line for
Exercise 2.

Use the time line below. Solve.

9:00 A.M.   Noon   3:00 P.M.   6:00 P.M.

5. Paul's baby sister goes to sleep at 4:00 P.M. She wakes up at 6:00 P.M. How long does the baby sleep?

_____ hours

6. Julia goes to a friend's house at noon. She comes home at 3:00 P.M. How long is Julia gone?

_____ hours

7. Jeff starts raking leaves at 11:00 A.M. He stops at 1:00 P.M. How long does Jeff rake leaves?

_____ hours

8. Mom and Carrie arrive at the shopping mall at 1:00 P.M. They leave at 5:00 P.M. How long are they at the mall?

_____ hours

Problem Solving

Solve. Draw or write to explain.

9. Mr. Norton writes the time for classes on the board.

Class	Time
Math	8:30 A.M.
Reading	9:30 A.M.
Music	11:30 A.M.

How long will reading class last?

_____ hours

TAKE HOME ACTIVITY • Ask your child how much time passes between 4:30 and 7:30. Have your child explain how he or she arrived at the answer.

Elapsed Time in Minutes

Essential Question How do you find the number of minutes between two times?

Model and Draw

You can use subtraction if the times are within the same hour.

Ken starts cleaning his room at 3:15 P.M. He finishes at 3:35 P.M. How long does it take Ken to clean his room?

$$\begin{array}{r} 35 \\ -15 \\ \hline 20 \end{array}$$

Starts at 3:15 P.M.   Ends at 3:35 P.M.

So it takes Ken __20__ minutes.

Share and Show

Subtract to solve. Show your work.

1. Leah starts eating lunch at 12:10 P.M. She finishes at 12:25 P.M. How long does it take for Leah to eat lunch?

_____

____ minutes

2. Kwan gets on the school bus at 8:10 A.M. He gets to school at 8:55 A.M. How long is Kwan's bus ride?

____

____ minutes

3. Carla takes her dog to the park at 2:05 P.M. She gets back at 2:40 P.M. How long does Carla walk her dog?

____

____ minutes

4. Ethan starts his spelling homework at 6:25 P.M. He finishes at 6:45 P.M. How long does Ethan work on his spelling?

____

____ minutes

Math Talk How could you check your answers by looking at a clock?

Subtract to solve. Show your work.

5. Mrs. Hall puts a pizza in the oven at 6:10 P.M. She takes it out at 6:30 P.M. How long does the pizza bake?

_____

_____ minutes

6. The reading test starts at 1:10 P.M. Everyone must stop at 1:25 P.M. How long do the children have to take their test?

_____ minutes

7. Kelly starts drawing at 8:15 P.M. She finishes her picture at 8:40 P.M. How long does Kelly draw?

_____

_____ minutes

8. Tony starts reading at 4:30 P.M. He stops reading at 4:45 P.M. How long does Tony read?

_____

_____ minutes

Problem Solving

Show how to use **subtraction to solve**.

9. Mr. West gets to the bus stop at 9:05 A.M. He looks at the bus schedule.

Bus Arrival Times
8:30 A.M.
9:30 A.M.
10:30 A.M.

How long will Mr. West need to wait for a bus?

_____ minutes

 TAKE HOME ACTIVITY • Have your child track how many minutes it would take to do math homework if he or she starts at 5:15 P.M. and stops at 5:45 P.M.

Name _____

Capacity • Nonstandard Units

Essential Question How can you measure how much a container holds?

Model and Draw

Use a scoop and rice to estimate and measure how much a can holds.

- Estimate how many scoops the can holds.
- Fill a scoop with rice or water.
- Pour it into the can.
- Repeat until the can is full. Keep track of the number of scoops.

Share and Show

How many scoops does the container hold? Estimate. Then measure.

Container	Estimate	Measure
1. mug	about _____ scoops	about _____ scoops
2. vase	about _____ scoops	about _____ scoops
3. paper cup	about _____ scoops	about _____ scoops

Math Talk   Explain how you can tell which of the containers on this page is the largest.

Getting Ready for Grade 3

two hundred eighty-one **P281**

How many scoops does the container hold?
Estimate. Then measure.

Container	Estimate	Measure
4. jar	about _____ scoops	about _____ scoops
5. milk carton	about _____ scoops	about _____ scoops
6. bowl	about _____ scoops	about _____ scoops

Problem Solving Real World

Solve.

7. The red bowl holds 5 scoops of rice. The blue bowl holds twice as much rice as the red bowl. How many scoops of rice do the two bowls hold in all?

_____ scoops in all

TAKE HOME ACTIVITY • Have your child use a paper cup to estimate how much various containers hold. Then check his or her estimate by measuring how much each container holds.

Describe Measurement Data

Essential Question What measurement data can a line plot show?

Model and Draw

A line plot shows data on a number line.

Each X on this line plot stands for the length of 1 desk.

Lengths of Our Desks in Inches

___12___ desks were measured.

Two desks are ___24___ inches long.

The longest desk is ___27___ inches long.

The shortest desk is ___21___ inches long.

Share and Show

Write 3 more sentences to describe what the line plot above shows.

1. _____

2. _____

3. _____

Math Talk   Suppose you measured another desk. If the desk was 23 inches long, how could you show this on the line plot above?

Lengths of Our Classroom Books in Inches

Use the line plot to answer the questions.

4. How many books are 9 and 10 inches in length?

_____ books

5. What is the difference in length between the shortest and longest book?

_____ inches

Write another question you can answer by looking at the line plot. Answer your question.

6. Question _____

_____

Answer _____

Problem Solving

7. Look at the table to the right. It shows Tom's books and their lengths. Add the data for the books to the line plot at the top of the page.

Book	Length
Reading	11 inches
Math	12 inches
Spelling	9 inches

 TAKE HOME ACTIVITY • Ask your child to explain how to read the line plot on this page.

Name _____

✓ Checkpoint

Write the time shown on the clock. Then write the time 1 hour before and 1 hour after.

1.

I hour before _____

I hour after _____

2.

I hour before _____

I hour after _____

2:00 P.M.   3:00 P.M.   4:00 P.M.   5:00 P.M.   6:00 P.M.   7:00 P.M.   8:00 P.M.

Use the time line above. Solve.

3. A movie begins at 2:00 P.M. It is over at 5:00 P.M. How long is the movie?

____ hours

4. Madison arrives at a friend's house at 3:00 P.M. She leaves at 7:00 P.M. How long does she stay?

____ hours

Subtract to solve. Show your work.

5. Will arrives at the library at 1:15 P.M.
He leaves at 1:50 P.M. How long is
Will at the library?

_____ minutes

---

6. Andrew begins reading at 3:20 P.M.
He stops reading at 3:45 P.M.
How long did Andrew read?

_____ minutes

How many scoops does the container hold? Estimate. Then measure.

7.

plastic cup

Estimate: about _____ scoops

Measure: about _____ scoops

---

8. What is the difference in height between the
shortest and tallest plants?

Heights of Plants in Inches

○   3 inches

○   4 inches

○   5 inches

○   6 inches

Fraction Models: Thirds and Sixths

Essential Question How can you identify thirds and sixths?

Model and Draw

__3__ equal parts or __3__ thirds

__6__ equal parts or __6__ sixths

__1__ part of 3 equal parts or
__1__ third

__1__ part of 6 equal parts or
__1__ sixth

Share and Show

Color the strips. Show two different ways to show 1 third.

1.

2.

Color the strips. Show two different ways to show 1 sixth.

3.

4.

Math Talk How are 3 thirds and 6 sixths alike?

Color the strips. Show two different ways to show 2 thirds.

5.

6.

Color the strips. Show two different ways to show 2 sixths.

7.

8.

Color the strips. Show two different ways to show 3 sixths.

9.

10.

Solve. Write or draw to explain.

11. A sub sandwich is cut into sixths. Tim eats two parts of the sandwich. How many parts are left?

_____ parts left

TAKE HOME ACTIVITY • Have your child draw a picture that shows a slice of cheese divided into thirds.

Fraction Models: Fourths and Eighths

Essential Question How can you identify **fourths** and **eighths**?

Model and Draw

__4__ equal parts or __4__ fourths

__8__ equal parts or __8__ eighths

__1__ part of 4 equal parts or

__1__ fourth

__1__ part of 8 equal parts or

__1__ eighth

Share and Show

Color the strips. Show two different ways to show I fourth.

1.

2.

Color the strips. Show two different ways to show I eighth.

3.

4.

Math Talk How are 4 fourths and 8 eighths alike?

Color the strips. Show two different ways to show 2 fourths.

5.

6.

Color the strips. Show two different ways to show 3 eighths.

7.

8.

Color the strips. Show two different ways to show 5 eighths.

9.

10.

Problem Solving

Solve. Write or draw to explain.

11. A loaf of bread is cut into eighths. Jake uses 2 parts to make his lunch. Fran uses 3 parts to make her lunch. How many parts of the loaf are left?

_____ parts left

TAKE HOME ACTIVITY • Have your child draw a picture to show a slice of cheese divided into fourths.

Compare Fraction Models

Essential Question How can you use fraction models to make comparisons?

Model and Draw

fourth	fourth	fourth	fourth

half	half

I fourth ⊖< I half

Share and Show

Color to show the fractions. Write <, =, or >.

1.

I **half**

half	half

2 fourths

fourth	fourth	fourth	fourth

I half ◯ 2 fourths

2.

I fourth

fourth	fourth	fourth	fourth

I eighth

eighth	eighth	eighth	eighth	eighth	eighth	eighth	eighth

I fourth ◯ I eighth

Math Talk Look at the strips above. Is I half greater than or less than 3 fourths? How do you know?

Color to show the fractions. Write <, =, or >.

3.

1 **third**	third	third	third

1 sixth	sixth	sixth	sixth	sixth	sixth	sixth

1 third 1 sixth

4.

3 sixths	sixth	sixth	sixth	sixth	sixth	sixth

1 half	half	half

3 sixths ◯ 1 half

Problem Solving Real World

Solve. Draw to show your answer.

5. Barry cut a cheese stick into halves and ate a half. Marcy cut a cheese stick into fourths and ate a fourth. Which child ate more cheese?

_____ ate more.

 TAKE HOME ACTIVITY • Ask your child to draw a picture that shows a square divided into fourths.

Concepts and Skills

Color the strips. Show two different ways to show 1 third.

1.

2.

Color the strips. Show two different ways to show 2 sixths.

3.

4.

Color the strips. Show two different ways to show 2 fourths.

5.

6.

Color the strips. Show two different ways to show 4 eighths.

7.

8.

Color to show the fractions. Write >, <, or =.

9. 1 half

half	half

3 fourths

fourth	fourth	fourth	fourth

1 half $\bigcirc$ **3 fourths**

---

10. 1 third

third	third	third

2 sixths

sixth	sixth	sixth	sixth	sixth	sixth

1 third $\bigcirc$ **2 sixths**

---

11. A pizza has 6 slices. Six friends share the pizza equally. What fraction of the pizza does each friend eat?

○ 1 third

○ 2 thirds

○ 1 sixth

○ 2 sixths